A year with Yours

Name	
Address	
Postcode	
Home phone	
Mobile phone	
Email	

In case of emergency, contact:

Name	
Telephone	

USEFUL CONTACTS

BANK	
BUILDING SOCIETY	
CHEMIST/PHARMACY	
CHIROPODIST	
COUNCIL	
CREDIT CARD EMERGENCY	
DENTIST	
DOCTOR	
ELECTRICIAN	
GARAGE	
HAIRDRESSER	
HOSPITAL	
LOCAL POLICE	
MILKMAN	
OPTICIAN	
PLUMBER	
SOLICITOR	
TAXI	
VET	

RENEWAL REMINDERS

	RENEWAL DATE	POLICY NUMBER	TELEPHONE
CAR INSURANCE			
CAR TAX			
MOT			
HOME INSURANCE			
TV LICENCE			
PET INSURANCE			
Yours SUBSCRIPTION			

THE YEAR AHEAD

A *new season blooms*

Did you know?
Most cherry blossom flowers are shades of white or pink, but you may see yellow or even green cherry blossom

A ROMANTIC ROAD TRIP

Blossom is one of spring's showstoppers, creating a magical scene as it falls like snow onto the ground. Venture to the Vale of Evesham in southern Worcestershire – a place of quirky rural charm – where 3,000 acres of orchards burst into colour each year, between the months of March and May. You can enjoy some of the prettiest sights and scents by following the 50-mile AA-signposted Blossom Trail – home to varieties of white plum, damson flower, white pear and pink apple trees.

◆ To book a guided coach tour with Dudley's Daybreaks, call 01386 792206 or visit www.dudleys-coaches.co.uk

BEST FOR BEACHCOMBING

With its sweeping sands and charming red-roofed cottages, Runswick Bay is one of the Yorkshire Coast's prettiest destinations. Just north of Whitby, its golden sands provide not only the perfect setting for a traditional bucket-and-spade day on the beach, but also one of the best beachcombing spots in Britain – especially during a spring tide. Ammonites and dinosaur footprints can be found all along the Jurassic rocks, as can semi-precious stones, shark eggs and historical artefacts, such as Second World War bullet casings. And just like any good beach, rock-pooling, sandcastle building, and walking are favourite pastimes here, too.

SAMPLE THE SEASON

Halfway down the border between Wales and England, you'll find pretty Ludlow with its half-timbered pubs and Georgian hotels. From May 7-9, visitors can enjoy the Ludlow Spring Festival. With the historical castle as its backdrop, the famous event focuses on beer, bread, bangers and classic cars. Guests can meet food producers and sample their delicious delicacies, plus there are free cookery sessions and activities for the grandchildren.
◆ **Call 01584 873957 or visit www.foodfestival.co.uk**

BLOOMING BRILLIANT

Down in West Sussex, the 11th Century Arundel Castle sees more than 80,000 colourful tulips burst into bloom during its annual Tulip Festival. Throughout the month of April, you can admire brightly coloured borders, a tulip labyrinth, beautiful shaped displays and botanical varieties in the quirky Stumpery - home to the upturned trunks of ancient trees. Other highlights include the dinky Persian Pearl tulip, at just 15cm tall, and the unusual-looking Parrot Negrita, with its extravagantly feathered deep purple petals. Inside the medieval mansion itself awaits nearly 1,000 years of history, with collections of fine furniture and works of art.
◆ **Call 01903 882173 or visit www.arundelcastle.org**

3 OF THE BEST... MARVELLOUS MAZES

You can find several mazes on the **Longleat Estate** in Wiltshire including the largest in Britain. It consists of nearly 1.75 miles of paths hedged by more than 16,000 8ft English yews that wind around a central observation tower. There are dozens of dead ends, plus six raised bridges that provide a bird's eye view of the horticultural creation. A fun afternoon for all the family.
◆ **Call 01985 844400**

Created around 1700 for William III, the **Hampton Court Palace Maze,** in Surrey, is the UK's oldest surviving hedge maze. A puzzle maze known for confusing and intriguing visitors over the centuries with its many twists, turns and dead ends.
◆ **Call 0333 320 6000**

The beautiful gardens at **Chatsworth House** in the Peak District are home to a circular English yew maze, planted with 1,209 trees in 1962. It features a long, straight ascent, called the Hundred Steps, which runs uphill from the maze, interrupted halfway along by a spectacular monkey puzzle tree.
◆ **Call 01246 565300**

A spring of fresh

CLIMB EV'RY MOUNTAIN

With its 'just-right' Goldilocks weather and spectacular sights of nature all around, spring is the perfect season to take to the hills. Promising a hearty work-out, you'll also be treated to some of the most jaw-dropping panoramic views around to reward your lack of puff at the top. Walking with a group such as **The Ramblers (02039613300/ www.ramblers.org.uk)** is a great way to meet like-minded souls around the country or find a local club at **www.uk hillwalking.com**. Once you feel more confident about how far you can walk, grab a map, sturdy walking boots and a friend and try a hill walk for beginners such as Ingleborough - the lowest of the three Yorkshire Peaks with top-of-the-world views over the Pennines - or Conic Hill overlooking Loch Lomond and the start of the Highlands.

LIVE 'THE GOOD LIFE'

British farms are brimming with new life this season so there's no better time to sign up for a hands-on farm holiday. If you've always liked the idea of living off the land and mucking in on the farm, find out what it's like for real on a volunteer placement with World Wide Opportunities on Organic Farms. You will be allocated a place on a working farm where you'll help out with day-to-day tasks. You don't need any prior farming knowledge, as your host, who'll also provide your accommodation, will teach you everything you need to know from feeding livestock to caring for crops. For more information write to: **WWOOF UK, PO Box 2207, Buckingham MK18 9BW or visit www.wwoof.org.uk**

starts

Do it for fun
Relive your school playground days and whittle your waist at the same time by teaching yourself how to hula-hoop! Try it in your living room or find your nearest hula-hooping class at **www.powerhoop.co.uk**

LEARN THE BIRDIE SONG

It's that time of year when our early morning routines are serenaded by a very special singsong, as Britain's birds croon their hearts out in the pursuit of love – a sound that has been shown to reduce our own stress and anxiety. Make the most of this free daily concert by sneaking outdoors about an hour before sunrise with a Thermos and blanket and see if you can train yourself to identify who's singing what. For example, birds such as cuckoos, curlews and chiffchaffs make a call that sounds like their name. Alternatively use the app Warblr (on Apple phones and Android) to record and identify the species that are singing.

STUDY FOR YOUR SUMMER HOLIDAY

It's prime season for booking overseas summer getaways, so why not do things a little different this year by challenging yourself to learning a little of the language of the country you're going to visit? Getting to grips with the lingo could not only help you get around a little easier and chat to the locals, it's also proven that language learning can improve your memory, help stave off dementia and even make your brain grow! To get started, look for local language classes - the Open University run lots **(call 0300 3035303 or visit www.open.ac.uk/ courses/languages)** or try a free online app such as DuoLingo (on iOS and Android). Top tip! Learning a language is easier if you practice with another person, so rope in a friend to learn with you.

◆ **If you like the idea of trying lots of new things, join the Yours FitMind50 challenge.** Encouraging you to try 50 new things of your choosing, whether that's experimenting with a new recipe, visiting somewhere new or joining a club, sign up to the challenge at www.fitmind50.co.uk and make friends in our supportive Fitmind50 group at facebook.com/groups/fitmind50

Yours FIT MIND 50

Marvellous magnolias

Iconic trees with unmatched elegance, bring magnolias into your garden to announce the arrival of spring, says Melissa Mabbitt

Magnolias never go out of style. The grand and gorgeous, goblet-shaped flowers adorn the otherwise bare, dark branches, lighting up the skies with pearly blossom. They are one of the first big statement flowers of the year to bloom, announcing the arrival of spring in style. They've been popular in gardens for decades, so you'll often see large and stately magnolias draped over garden walls and fences around older houses, but there are many that are bijou enough to fit into small plots, and their chic blooms complement even the most modern of garden designs.

Magnolia flowers can be snow-white, a warm coppery-cream (it's no coincidence that 'magnolia' is one of the nation's most popular paint shades), plush-pink, rich-plum or even golden in colour. They often have an alluring scent, too, with zesty citrus notes that remind you of a freshly baked lemon tart. As spring turns into summer, the thick waxy petals fold away from the flowers and drop to the floor to make a blanket of bumper-sized confetti.

The flowers are not the only gorgeous quality magnolias possess. They have large shiny foliage that can look almost tropical, even in the most English of country gardens. Some are evergreen and have leaves with a leathery, waxy shine, making them ideal for adding lush greenery to your garden through winter and spring. Meanwhile, those that lose their leaves in the winter season reveal an architectural network of branches. Throughout late winter, you will notice the big and promising furry flower buds decorating the tips of the bare branches. The lining of each bud protects the bloom inside from frost and snow until they can unfurl when the weather warms up, popping out to say a cheerful hello out of the clutches of winter.

CHOOSE THE PERFECT ONE

Magnolias range in size, so it's important to choose the right one for the space you have. They tend to grow sideways as much as upwards, so check the growing width or 'spread' on the label before you buy. There are plenty of magnolias for small gardens. 'Caerhays Surprise' is a good choice, reaching about 4m after ten years, with gorgeous, deep-pink waterlily-like flowers.

However, it's still possible to accommodate a larger magnolia if you've fallen in love with its flowers and scent, because it can take decades for them to reach their full size. This means most of their lifetime they'll stay within comfortable bounds. Silky pink-flowered 'Apollo' is one such larger tree, growing to an eventual 5m so slowly that it's easy to accommodate.

HOW TO GROW

It's important that magnolias get the right kind of soil and light, or their leaves can start to yellow. They need a warm, sheltered and sunny spot and rich, organic compost.

You can plant a magnolia at any time of the year, but spring or autumn are best. Weed the area where you are going to plant and dig a hole that's twice as wide and the same depth as the pot the roots are in. Place them in the hole and make sure the top of the compost from the pot is level with the top of the surrounding soil. Fill the sides of the hole with compost, firming it in as you go. Pour in half a can of water, then put a thick layer of compost around the plant and repeat this every spring.

3 OF THE BEST FOR SCENT

'Heaven Scent'
The elegant, upright pink flowers have a rich, honey scent. £17.99 thompson-morgan.com

'Leonard Messel'
The sweetly scented blooms have starry, baby-pink and white petals. £24.99 crocus.co.uk

'Colossus'
Highly fragrant white flowers appear in spring and summer. £25 burncoose.co.uk

Keyring cuties

Never lose your house keys again with these cute-as-a-button clay bead keyrings that would also make a lovely handmade gift

MATERIALS:
Scissors
Sewing needles
White clay
Acrylic paint
Porcelain pens
Sandpaper block
Satin ribbon
Gloss finish glue
Keyrings
Thread in same colour as ribbon

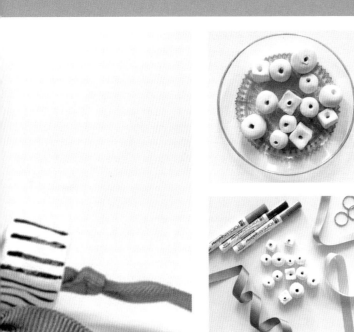

1 Taking the clay out of the packaging, separate it into a dozen or so little balls. Then mould it into your chosen shape. You can technically choose any shape you like but round or square will probably work best. Use a needle or cocktail stick to make holes through the centre of your clay pieces.

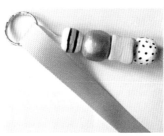

2 When all the pieces of clay are complete, leave them in a cool, dry space and allow them to completely dry. This will take around 2-3 days. Keep checking on your clay to see how they are drying as you may need to turn them over every once in a while.

3 Once the clay is dry and stiffened, you can start decorating your pieces. Use acrylic paint or experiment with fancy patterns using the porcelain pens. You can do any design you like: spots, stripes, block colours. Feel free to get creative but think about how each bead on your keyring compliments the rest.

4 Once the paint is dry, choose a length of coloured satin ribbon and thread at least four beads onto this. Tie a knot at the end and snip off the excess ribbon in a neat way that leaves the beads with a pretty little tail.

5 Finally, thread the rest of the ribbon through the keyring and in a thread the same colour as your ribbon, sew tightly across the top, securing the ribbon to the keyring. Leave a small lip and cut the end of the ribbon neatly. All done - simply attach to your keys or a handbag for a pretty accessory.

By That's So Gemma for Hobbycraft.co.uk

Hello sunshine!

Did you know? Llamas are often mistaken for alpacas but a key way to tell them apart is that llamas are twice as big and have much longer ears than their alpaca cousins

COUNTRYSIDE COMPANIONS

For an outdoor experience with a difference this summer, animal lovers should certainly book a trek with Nidderdale Llamas. Matched up with your very own four-legged furry companion, you are then accompanied on a stroll through their picturesque Nidderdale countryside, an Area of Outstanding Natural Beauty in North Yorkshire.

Their unique personalities are sure to keep you amused along the way and some may even talk back to you with a gentle hum. Back on the farm, there are other animals to meet and greet - including rabbits, guinea pigs, chinchillas, ferrets and ponies.

◆ **Call 01423 711052 or visit www.nidderdalellamas.org**

A PIECE OF PARADISE

The oriental-themed Peasholm Park in Scarborough offers a wonderland of streams and waterfalls, little bridges and mystical gardens - an ideal setting for a summer day out. Whether you row, paddle or pedal, there are lots of ways to take a trip around the boating lake. It's the town's local park and three times a week between May and September, a naval warfare event opens fire - the Battle of Peasholm. For the last 80 years, droves of tourists and local residents have come to witness the sailors potting shots at one another.
◆ **Visit www.discoveryorkshirecoast.com**

THEATRE UNDER THE STARS

Carved into the granite cliffs high above Porthcurno cove in Cornwall is the marvellous Minack Theatre. A stone amphitheatre featuring grassy terraces and sub-tropical gardens overlooking a spectacular panorama, the summer theatre season runs from May to September, showcasing drama, musicals and opera. Visit during the day to enjoy sweeping vistas of the Atlantic azure and return for an evening performance, when moonlight glimmers on the sea and lights of an occasional fishing vessel can be seen flickering in the distance.
◆ **Call 01736 810181 or visit www.minack.com**

SLOW THE PACE

The North Norfolk Railway is one of the greatest heritage railways Britain has to offer, taking you on a breathtakingly scenic ride from Sheringham along the coast to Weybourne then inland through the beautiful heathland to Holt. Lovingly run by volunteers, the journey will take you back to a gentler age. You'll visit three Victorian stations, including Sheringham, where you'll find a waiting room unchanged since the Fifties, and a restored signal box. The volunteers also put on numerous special events throughout the summer months - from Forties weekends to beer festivals - so be sure to check the calendar.
◆ **Call 01263 820800 or visit www.nnrailway.co.uk**

3 OF THE BEST...
OUTDOOR SWIMMING SPOTS

Plymouth's superb **Tinside Lido** boasts a classic art-deco design complete with fountains. Filled with fresh, unheated seawater it makes for a beautiful, if bracing swim. After taking a dip, dry off on the sun terrace, which commands a spectacular vantage point overlooking the blue waves of Plymouth Hoe.
◆ **Call 01752 261915**

Open daily between late May and early September, **Stonehaven Open Air Pool** in Aberdeen offers brilliant fun rain or shine, in the day or even at night. The saltwater of this Olympic-sized, open-air, heated pool is taken from Stonehaven Bay, and is cleaned and heated to offer family fun, as well as quiet swims and - for those who dream of swimming under the stars - late-night swimming sessions in summer.
◆ **Call 01569 762134**

A jewel in the crown of the Lincolnshire countryside, Woodhall Spa's **Jubilee Park** features recreation grounds, rose gardens, a bandstand and a heated pool that sits in its own immaculately manicured grounds. You'll also find a pool for little ones, a slide and a fountain.
◆ **Call 01526 353478**

FESTIVAL CITY

Since 1947, Edinburgh has boasted one of the UK's biggest arts festivals throughout the summer months with the International Festival and the Fringe. Walk down the Royal Mile come summertime and you'll jostle with everyone from knife-throwing uni-cyclists to bagpiping buskers, aria-belting opera singers to contortionists, enticing you to buy a ticket for their shows.
◆ **Call 0131 529 7970 or visit www.edinburghfestivalcity.com**

A summer to be

FORAGE FOR FRUIT

Summer is the perfect time to grab your wicker basket and head off for a spot of wild berry picking. Take a trip to one of the hundreds of Pick Your Own (PYO) farms all around the country where you're actively encouraged to peep under the strawberry bushes and go rummaging for raspberries (to find your nearest, visit **www.pick yourownfarms.org.uk**)

SCRAPBOOK YOUR STORIES

Make this an extra-special summer by documenting what you and the family get up to. Scrapbooking is a lovely way to preserve memories, for now and the future, and is a great activity to do with the grandchildren. Start by writing a list of all the things you want to get up to this summer, whether it's going to the seaside, exploring the local park or watching an outdoor movie. Then take time every so often to write about what happened, stick in photos or add mementoes such as pressed flowers you found on walks or shells from the beach. In years to come, this scrapbook will be a treasured portal back to this happy summer past. Alternatively, if you'd like something you can share more directly with others, how about setting up an online blog documenting your adventures. **Wordpress.com** or **weebly.com** are good bloggings sites to get you started and you can simply treat it like an online diary, adding entries and photos whenever you like.

challenged

Do it for fun

Rewind to the Eighties and get your skates on by joining a local roller-skating club. To find your nearest, call 01635 877322 or visit **www.fars.co.uk**

WILD FOR THE OUTDOORS....

Love walking? Make more of your daily stroll by incorporating new hobbies while you put one foot in front of the other. Geocaching is an up-and-coming hobby that's best described as a treasure hunt for grown-ups. The way it works is this: there are millions of different-sized containers – known as geocaches – hidden all over the world, including many near you. To find them, use a smartphone to create an account on **geocaching.com** and follow the instructions to find the nearest geocache. Once you've located it, write your name in a logbook kept inside the cache and then look for the next one. Some are kept in hard-to-find places meaning you're likely to discover new places in your local area, all while walking miles.

TALK TO THE ANIMALS

Embrace your inner Dr Dolittle by signing up this summer to volunteer with animals. So many local rescue centres and charities are crying out for volunteers so if you have even a few hours' free time in a week, this could be a great way to make a difference while making yourself feel good, too. The RSPCA is regularly looking for cat socialiser volunteers to spend time cuddling and playing with their rescue cats and kittens while they're waiting to be rehomed (write to **RSPCA Advice Team, Wilberforce Way, Southwater, Horsham, West Sussex RH13 9RS** or visit **www.rspca.org.uk**). Or if you're more of a dog person, **the Guide Dogs charity** often needs puppy walkers to help tiny pups become life-changing dogs **(call 0118 983 5555 or visit www.guidedogs.org.uk).**

Yours

FIT MIND 50

◆ If you like the idea of trying lots of new things, join the **Yours FitMind50** challenge. Encouraging you to try 50 new things of your choosing, whether that's experimenting with a new recipe, visiting somewhere new or joining a club, sign up to the challenge at www.fitmind50.co.uk and make friends in our supportive Fitmind50 group at facebook.com/groups/fitmind50

In the pink

Plant a fragrant rose then sit back, relax and drink in the scent of summer, says Louise Curley

No flower better conjures an image of a perfect British summer's day than a pink rose. Long a staple in traditional cottage-garden borders, these beauties are fast becoming a must-have in the most modern of gardens, softening landscaping and adding a summer scent to rival any expensive perfume.

Flowering profusely from early summer in a whole suite of colours, from pastel peaches to snowy white, punchy yellow to deep crimson, they're the most charming of companions for those long summer evenings spent in the garden.

The Hybrid Tea Rose is definitely one of the most common to brighten up a traditional garden, with its bounteous blooms and vast selection of shades. Meanwhile, shrub roses are great for a larger garden. The real show-offs of the rose world, they'll draw all eyes as they sprawl out to fill the space. Nevertheless, behind their flashy exterior, there's a hardy spirit that will see them through winter, making them a good-value choice.

For smaller gardens, pick miniature varieties that will thrive in a pot on the patio or bushy shrubs to fill garden borders. Or if you fancy a whole wall of scent, rampant ramblers will cover the side of a house in no time, while climbers will be happy gently scrambling over a pergola.

And when the summer sun withdraws at the end of the season, you can bring the beauty indoors by taking a few delicate cuttings in late summer and autumn, brightening up your rooms with its pretty looks and endless scent.

HOW TO PLANT

Roses can be planted at any time of the year as long as it isn't frosty, the soil isn't waterlogged and there isn't a drought. Start by digging a hole twice as deep and wide as the container or roots. Tip in a bag of multi-purpose compost and mix into the soil with a fork. Scatter mycorrhizal fungi (£3.95 davidaustinroses.co.uk) onto the roots and into the planting hole. This will encourage the roots to grow, so the plant can produce more flowers. Carefully tip the plant from the pot and position in the hole. Fill the hole with compost and firm in place with your hands. Water thoroughly using a full can.

KEEP YOUR ROSES HAPPY

Water newly planted roses once a week in spring and autumn and every other day in summer. Once established, water once a week in summer. Use five litres of water for container roses and shrub roses, and ten litres for thirstier climbing roses. Water at the base to avoid splashing leaves as this can cause fungal diseases.

Snip off fading flowers so the plant puts its energy into growing new flowers, rather than seed heads. It's best if you can cut back to where the flower appeared from the stem.

Prune in later winter or early spring. First remove any dead, dying, damaged or diseased stems. Cut the remaining stems back by a third. If it's a climbing rose, snip off any stems that are growing away from the trellis. Use soft twine to tie the remaining main stems onto the support. Shorten any old flowering shoots that grow off the main stems to approximately 15cm long.

THREE RADIANT ROSES TO TRY

'Baby Masquerade'
Compact and low growing, the peachy and yellow petals are evocative of sunset. £10.99, grovesnurseries.co.uk

'Chippendale'
Quintessentially pink and voluptuous blooms will be out from May to September £25.40 lubera.co.uk

'Albertine'
A climber with silver-pink, sweetly perfumed petals. £19.99 crocus.co.uk

A box of treasures

Handy tip:
Press your pieces of fabric before starting your project to make the fabric easier to work with

Keep all your precious mementoes or little household knickknacks safe in this pretty fabric storage box

By Paula Milner for Hobbycraft.co.uk

MATERIALS:

Scissors
Dress making pins
Tape measure
Cotton fat quarters cut to the following sizes:
4 x Outer rectangles
6.3 x 8.7in (16 x 22cm)
1 x Outer square
6.3 x 6.3in (16 x 16cm)
4 x Inner rectangles
6.3 x 8.7in (16 x 22cm)
1 x Inner square
6.3 x 6.3in (16 x 16cm)
Sewing thread
Iron-on interfacing 1m x 1m

1 Pick two contrasting fabrics from your fat quarters - one for the inner layer and one for the outer - and cut into the measurements indicated in the Materials box, left.

2 Cut the interfacing to size and iron on to your inner fabric shapes as per the packet instructions. Each piece will need to be cut 1cm smaller than each shape to allow for the seams.

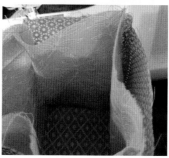

3 Start sewing your inner rectangles right sides together until you have all four rectangles together in a row. Then fold the sides together so that you join it into a cube - with the pattern facing inwards - and sew up. Now sew your bottom square piece onto your cube with a 1cm seam allowance.

4 Repeat the process of joining the sides into a cube on your outer rectangles and attach the bottom square - remembering to sew on the wrong side of the fabric. Turn out the right way. Insert your inner layer inside your outer layer.

5 Fold the inner layer inwards and sew in a stitch of your choice. Repeat with the outer layer, folding over the same amount of fabric. Then holding both layers of fabric fold the top outwards to reveal the contrasting patterns.

Fields of gold

HEAVENLY HEATHLAND

The New Forest in Hampshire transforms over autumn, with great swathes of rich colours and crisp atmospheric mornings. September brings vibrant pink and purple heather, contrasting with green bracken and yellowing silver birch leaves. Ancient oaks, beech and sweet chestnut trees display canopies of rich autumnal hues of gold and red, as fungi starts to emerge on the floor beneath them. The forest is well known for its animal populations and it won't be long before you cross paths with some of the 5,000 semi-wild ponies who roam freely here. Visit in October and you could even spot one of the 600 pigs who are let loose to snuffle up acorns and chestnuts.

Did you know?
The New Forest was first created by William the Conqueror in 1079 as a hunting preserve. Today's it's home to 700 wild flower species, about a third of Britain's total

RAISE A GLASS

British wine has come a long way in recent years, winning numerous international accolades, tempting even the most discerning of drinkers There are a number of beautiful vineyards across the UK where you can volunteer to help come harvest time. Look forward to leafy, sun-dappled fields of vines, cheerful camaraderie with workers and fellow volunteers, and maybe even a glass of the local wine and a hearty lunch. You'll be shown the ropes on the day – and once you know where to cut the stem, you're set.

◆ To find out if there are any opportunities near you visit www.winecellardoor.co.uk

ROAM LIKE ROYALTY

Hever Castle is a beautiful sight to behold as the autumn sun lights up the vivid Boston ivy that adorns its front walls. Former childhood home of Anne Boleyn, this double-moated medieval fort is a brilliant bolthole for budding historians and hopeless romantics alike. Step back into the medieval era as you wander panelled rooms furnished with a fine collection of furniture, antiques, Tudor paintings, tapestries and treasures. If the weather permits, pull on your walking boots to stroll through 125 acres of glorious grounds, including the award-winning gardens and a lovely 38-acre lake.

◆ Call 01732 865224 or visit www.hevercastle.co.uk

A KALEIDOSCOPE OF COLOUR

Bodnant Garden in Conwy, North Wales is like a firework display of crimson, amber and gold in autumn, as the glowing leaves of trees and shrubs, ripening fruit and berries and late flowering plants put on a show. Set in a stunning location overlooking Snowdonia's Carneddau mountains, it's so much more than just a garden, offering guided walks and lots of nature-inspired activities for youngsters. Other highlights include striking sweet chestnut trees, a waterfall and a deep valley framed by towering trees.
◆ **Call 01492 650460 or visit www.nationaltrust.org.uk/bodnant-garden**

TAKE YOUR PICK

The heat of summer has its afterglow in the colours and tastes of autumn, making it one of foraging's core seasons. This activity of finding, gathering and harvesting wild foods is a rewarding way to stay active, connect with nature and learn more about where your food comes from. Woods, hedgerows, fields and even seabeds are brimming with wild foods that are perfectly safe to pick and eat – if you know what you're looking for. Wild Food UK runs foraging courses across the country, taking you on walks to help you identify plants, fruits and mushrooms.
◆ **Call 01981 590604 or visit www.wildfooduk.com**

3 OF THE BEST... ANCIENT MONUMENTS

English Heritage-managed **Avebury Henge** is one of the largest surviving ceremonial sites of Neolithic Britain, dating from about 2850 BC. Inside the henge are two smaller stone circles, which, unlike Stonehenge, visitors can explore freely.
◆ **Call 0370 333 1181**

The **Ring of Brodgar** is arguably the most iconic symbol of Orkney's prehistoric past. Its tall, slender, tablet-shaped stones are arranged in perfect circles and are part of a UNESCO World Heritage Site.
◆ **Call 01856 841815**

Set against the wonderful backdrop of Helvellyn and High Seat, the 40-odd standing stones of the circle at **Castlerigg**, Cumbria (above), are Late Neolithic or early Bronze Age and perhaps the most dramatically sited of all British stone circles. Managed by English Heritage.
◆ **Call 0370 333 1181**

An autumn of

NURTURE LITTLE BOOK WORMS

If you love nothing better than getting lost in a good book, why not share your passion for stories by volunteering to help children learn to read this back-to-school season? The children's reading charities **Beanstalk (call 0207 729 4087 or visit www. beanstalkcharity.org. uk)** and **School Readers (call 01234 924111** or visit **www.schoolreaders.org)** are always looking for eager volunteers to help spark a love of literature in little ones. You don't need any specific qualifications, just the will to make reading fun and a few hours' spare time each week.

A GOLDEN TIME TO PAINT

From fiery reds to pretty purples, with all the beautiful colours of nature around this autumn, it's a perfect time to channel your artistic side and learn how to paint what you see outside. Many colleges and universities run evening art classes for adults or else **CraftCourses** could help you find one-day courses (call 01239 805080 or visit **www.craftcourses. com**). Otherwise, a cheap and easy way to start is to buy a simple watercolour set and a sketchbook and just experiment with capturing what you see. If you're struggling, **YouTube** has lots of free online tutorials showing you how to master the basics, from how to work out perspective to a simple way to draw a tree.

adventures

DISCOVER YOUR FAMILY TREE

Make the most of the chillier weather calling you inside to do some digging into your ancestry. Start by interviewing your family about what they know about your ancestors and use that to draw up a simple family tree on paper. Search for birth, marriage and death certificates using the **general register office (03001231837/www.gro.gov. uk)** and visit your library to find other resources. **www.ancestry.co.uk** and **www.findmypast. co.uk** can help you find census records, while you can often find parish records such as baptisms, marriages and burials at your county archive. While you're searching, consider joining your local family history society which will have lots more advice as well as giving you the chance to meet other people doing some detective work into their own history.

IN THE SADDLE

See the autumn colours from a whole new perspective by going whistling through carpets of golden leaves on two wheels this autumn. Cycling has so many benefits from weight loss to improving your mood, and it's so easy to get started. If you've not been on a bike for a while, you could try e-biking where an electronic motor helps power you further and reduces the strain on your joints. Alternatively, look at hiring a bike in your local area or while on holiday to give it a try and see how you find it. Some of the best cycling routes for beginners include Rutland Water in the Midlands, the Norbury loop in Shropshire and the London East End loop. You may also benefit from joining a local cycling club to give you the support and motivation to ride regularly. These groups are often associated with bike shops so ask the staff at your local shop if they can help you.

Do it for fun
Go all Robin Hood in the woods by taking up archery - a great form of exercise that's fun too. To find your nearest archery club **call Archery GB on 01952677888 or visit www.archerygb. org**

◆If you like the idea of trying lots of new things, join the **Yours FitMind50** challenge. Encouraging you to try 50 new things of your choosing, whether that's experimenting with a new recipe, visiting somewhere new or joining a club, sign up to the challenge at www.fitmind50.co.uk and make friends in our supportive Fitmind50 group at facebook.com/groups/fitmind50

Zest and zing

As the days grow gloomy, bring your garden to life with flowers and foliage in bright gaudy green hues, says Melissa Mabbitt

Whether you decide to dot your garden with bright splashes or add a solid block of colour, a dash of this exuberant acidic tone will make your garden a happier place during the cooler months of the year.

We're used to green being a calming, restful colour that's easy on the eye, but fresh bright greens are uplifting too, thought to make us feel recharged and calm at the same time. These gaudy greens are guaranteed to bring life to your outside space.

Choose the right greens and when you look out on to your garden you'll be rewarded by a splash of vibrance on even the greyest day. Some varieties, such as euphorbias, look great all year round, making them a great choice for linking the seasons.

The green tones of emerald and chartreuse lime and moss will throw a curveball of contrast into your garden, instantly creating a modern look.

And as green is usually the background colour of our outside spaces, making it the star of the show, instead of the usual filler makes a real statement. It's useful, too, to illuminate shady spots at their darkest on wintry days, especially if you pop them in neutral coloured pots.

What's more, because greens are so synonymous with nature, they magically work well with every other colour meaning you can plant it into any colour scheme.

With all this in mind, it's no wonder many top modern designers love to bring quirky greens into their stylish gardens, while leading flower-arrangers flock to get hold of these emerald gems.

Hellebores are one of the best for a deep green blast of colour all year round and come in all kinds of shapes from striking stars to flouncy petals with frills. You can even get hold of some exotic varieties with splashes and spots like orchids.

GO EXOTIC

Greens can bring a taste of the tropics to your back garden with the help of euphorbias. The frilled green stems add cheer all year round and euphorbia's distinctive shape adds a striking architectural note which is eye-catching in winter. It looks particularly stunning outlined against a wall or fence.

One of the easiest plants to grow, euphorbias do well whatever the conditions. Although they do best in free-draining soil, they are equally happy in sandy or clay conditions. They thrive in wet winters and hot summers alike, making them one of the unfussiest plants around. Leave them to sprawl through a border as most varieties don't need staking. Give them a quick tidy-up if they start to look tatty.

PRETTY PLEASURES

One of the prettiest plants around, the soft velvety fan-shaped leaves of the Alchemilla Mollis have scalloped edges that add a gorgeous, frothy effect to your garden. The large lacy sprays of tiny star-like flowers that top the fabulous foliage are chartreuse-coloured, honey scented and nectar rich to attract pollinating insects. Grown mainly as an ornamental garden plant, it's a great foil for more colourful blooms as it works with everything.

Handily, too, when the autumn rains inevitably fall, that's when this plant comes into its own. Pleats and folds in the leaves are slightly downy so catch the raindrops and hold them, creating a sparkling display in the sunlight. But it's not just rain the Alchemilla Mollis can withstand. Happy in sun or partial shade, it's not fussy about soil and will even thrive in heavy clay.

THREE OF THE PRETTIEST HELLEBORES

'Winter Bells'
Perfect for porches and covered patios, flowers from October. £10.95, sarahraven.com

'Corsican Hellebore'
These easy-care plants look fragile but can withstand anything. £16.99 crocus.co.uk

'Green Dream'
Makes a stylish table display used fresh or dried. £10 hayloft.co.uk

A hug in a mug

LET'S STAY HOME

you
&
A CUP O

As the autumn days get cooler, enjoy a comforting cuppa in a charming and unique personalised mug

1 Stick the Washi tape in a straight line around your enamel mug to make guidelines that will help you write in a straight line. To do the same lettering as pictured, put Washi tape halfway down the mug, and write the top line above and the bottom line below in your chosen colour of marker pen.

2 Now start your floral pattern in a different colour pen. You can draw flowers however you like, but an easy way is to use this simple four-petal shape around the whole mug that makes a lovely ditsy floral pattern.

3 In a third colour add little leaves using a teardrop shape that can be as big or as small as you like. Use the colour that you previously used for your writing to add dots to the middle of your flowers.

4 Alternatively you can create a leafy motif like that shown left, using whatever colours you fancy. It doesn't have to be perfect! Add dots in a different colour pen to give the impression of berries.

5 Leave the mugs to dry for 24 hours. Once dry, place on an ovenproof dish and bake in the oven at 160 degrees C for 40 minutes to secure the design. You can also paint on a clear varnish to make sure the design stays put.

By Becki Clark for Hobbycraft.co.uk

MATERIALS:
Plain enamel mugs or cups
Washi tape
Marker pens (in a variety of colours)

Season's greetings

FIELDS OF FROST

The National Nature Reserve Wicken Fen in Cambridgeshire is a magical sight on a crisp winter's day, as ice twinkles on the trees and reedbeds while steam appears from the noses of the resident Konik ponies and Highland cattle. The all-weather Boardwalk Trail offers a good walk even in cold weather. Along the way, you'll find hides for watching birds and a pretty old windpump – a throwback to the peat-digging industry that was once widespread in the Fens. Wicken Fen was the first nature reserve to be owned by the National Trust, with the first land purchased in 1899.
◆ **Call 01353 720274**

WATERFALL MAGIC

Winter creates the magical backdrop for exploring the mature woodland of Glenariff Forest Park in County Antrim, Northern Ireland, with freezing waterfalls and open, frosted moorland. Way markers lead to a spectacular spray-swept boardwalk over a series of tumbling rapids and thunderous falls. Look out for darting red squirrels which have made their home along the dripping lichens and fragrant ferns. For views without the steep steps, parking is available at Laragh Lodge, where two of the biggest cascades can be accessed in just five minutes by foot.
◆ **Call 0282 175 8221**

Winter days out

MID-WINTER TROPICS

Most gardens go into hibernation at this time of year – but Kew Royal Botanic Gardens are just as spectacular in winter. Visitors can retreat from the elements and enjoy a taste of the tropics in the Temperate House – home to 1,500 species of plants from around the world.

Experience the magic of Christmas at Kew, when archways glitter and vivid colours light up the famous glasshouse. It's the place to be for seasonal festivities, with plenty of mulled wine to try and delicious culinary treats.
◆ **Call 0208 332 5655 or visit www.kew.org**

VIKING TRADITIONS

With oodles of old-world charm, historic architecture and quirky tearooms, few places rival York when it comes to cosy city breaks. Take a guided tour and see highlights such as York Minster Cathedral and The Shambles – or even join a winter ghost walk if you dare! Time your visit between mid-November and late-December and you can enjoy the sights and scents of the season at the city's annual Christmas Festival. Or visit in February when the city celebrates its Viking ancestry with traditional 'Jolablot' celebrations that were held to herald the coming of spring.
◆ **Visit www.visityork.org**

3 OF THE BEST... OBSERVATION TOWERS

Experience Brighton's best views with **British Airways i360**. Gently glide up to 450ft in the glass viewing pod to enjoy 360° views of Brighton, the South Downs and the East Sussex coastline. Spot the city's landmarks, artwork on rooftops, wind farms and the expansive stretch of coast all the way from the Seven Sisters cliffs to the Isle of Wight.
◆ **Call 0333 772 0360**

Radio City Tower offers the unique opportunity to admire Liverpool's most iconic landmarks and enjoy breath-taking views of the Wirral, North Wales, Lancashire and even as far as Snowdonia on clearer days.
◆ **Call 0151 472 6800**

See London's stunning skyline from the UK's tallest sculpture, **the Orbit Tower**. The magnificent looping structure is an iconic symbol of The Queen Elizabeth Olympic Park and the London 2012 Games where you can discover sights including Big Ben, St Paul's Cathedral and the O2. For those with a head for heights, the tower also features the world's longest and tallest tunnel slide... if you dare!
◆ **Call 0333 800 8099**

A winter of wonder

WISH UPON A STAR

With crisp, chilly nights bringing all the constellations out to play, winter is the perfect time to try stargazing. You don't need any snazzy equipment to start, just head out into the night to a spot out of the direct glare of light at least an hour and a half after sunset. To help you get a sense of what you're looking at, refer to Philip's Stargazing Month-by-Month Guide to the Night Sky or download the Google Sky app which allows you to point your phone at the sky to work out constellations. For the best place to see stars head to one of the UK's Dark Sky Reserves on Exmoor, the Brecon Beacons, Cranborne Chase in Salisbury and Moore's Reserve in the South Downs. Find the best stargazing spots local to you at **darkskydiscovery.org.uk**

MAKE CHILD'S PLAY OF YOUR EVENINGS

With the weather so chilly now, it's easy to find yourself in front of the telly each night. But why not change things up by making at least one evening a week a TV-free zone. Instead channel your inner child and get out the board games to play with your family. If you're bored of the usual Monopoly, change things up with a game such as Linkee where you have to find the common connection between words, or Ticket To Ride, a beautifully illustrated game of strategy taking you on a rail adventure across Europe.

Do it for fun
Belt out well-known hits somewhere other than the shower and make friends by joining the nationwide Rock Choir. To find your nearest call **01252 714276** or visit **www.rockchoir.com**

DANCE THE NIGHT AWAY

It's Strictly Come Dancing season, but it's not just famous faces who are putting on their dancing shoes and learning something new. Dancing has been shown to help with your heart health, balance, strength and so many other things. If you like the ballroom and Latin numbers you see on Strictly, try Fitsteps, a nationwide exercise class based on the show (to find your nearest class call **01242 374029** or visit **www.fitsteps.co.uk**). Or if you love the gracefulness of ballet – which incidentally is a great workout for your body's core muscles – try the ballet-based exercise trend Barre (find your nearest class at **www.barreconcept.co.uk**).

START A BOOK CLUB

Book clubs are one of the best ways to make new friends in your area while giving you the perfect excuse to sneak away from the hassles of everyday life to lose yourself in a book. There are already hundreds of them around (ask at your local book shop or visit **readinggroups.org** to find your nearest) but it is easy enough to start your own. Just gather a group of no more than eight people together and find a place to meet, whether that's your home or the corner of a café. Meet every 4-6 weeks and take it in turns to pick a book. To keep costs down, encourage members to borrow library books or buy the Kindle version. Ahead of the session think about key questions to ask or fun activities you could do, such as seeing the film adaptation of the book together.

◆ If you like the idea of trying lots of new things, join the **Yours FitMind50** challenge. Encouraging you to try 50 new things of your choosing, whether that's experimenting with a new recipe, visiting somewhere new or joining a club, sign up to the challenge at www.fitmind50.co.uk and make friends in our supportive Fitmind50 group at facebook.com/groups/fitmind50

Yours
FIT MIND
50

Let it snow

Using a simple palette of all-white snowy flowers creates a stunning winter garden of moonlit moods, says Melissa Mabbitt

A growing trend in modern gardens is to shun the usual spectrum of bright blooms and opt instead for flowers in plain, simple white. The effect isn't as stark as you might imagine as by removing all that attention-grabbing colour, you notice the shapes and textures of the flowers all the more. You're left with a soothing space that couldn't be more modern.

White may be pure, but it's far from a simple colour. White flowers range in shades from creamy, almost lemon-tinted, to silvery grey or blue-tinted ice and, with an entirely pale palette, your senses will soon start to notice these subtle differences between shades. They will create a patchwork of snowy hues in your garden, sparkling in the midday sun and glowing in the dusky evening. All flowers look fab in summer sunshine, but white blooms come into their own as darkness falls, their pale shades popping out from the night-time gloom.

You'll need to be fully devoted to your theme to make it work well as just one purple tip can ruin the effect, but that doesn't mean there's no room for creativity or experimentation.

We've seen lots of wild and magical woodland gardens in all the top garden shows lately, with white flowers shining from dappled shady spaces. Sharper but still effortlessly chic, sun-bleached Hamptons-style gardens are also bang on-trend, their laid-back elegance perfectly complemented by calm and relaxing white flowers and accessories.

HOW TO MAKE IT WORK

Pared-back colour means you can focus on form. For the best result, vary the shapes of the plants, with spikes, pom-poms, star and bell-shaped blooms. Create contrasts of height, too, so your eye alights from one place to another, always finding something to delight in.

Support the stars of your show with a pale backdrop. Silver and grey leaves and white bark and stems should all play a part in the design. Using pale stone, paint and accessories will hone the look. These elements will also mean that the white theme continues throughout the year, even when flowers are few and far between in winter. And don't scrimp on lush green foliage. All those bleached-out blooms need a strong skeleton of green planting to look their best.

A PLAN FOR ALL SEASONS

It's easy to fill your space with blousy white blooms in summer, but a little planning will mean there's plenty of pale to pack a punch all year-round. Right now, as we descend into the frosty days of winter, the silvery bark of multi-stemmed birch trees (£59.99, ornamental-trees.co.uk) look fabulous, as do the otherworldly white stems of ghost bramble (£14.50, burncoose.co.uk) and the silver-grey leaves of cardoon (£5.99, crocus.co.uk) and Russian sage (£7.99 crocus.co.uk). All these will reflect the moonlight on clear, starry nights, so you can enjoy them on short days. Try daffodil 'Thalia' (£3.20 avonbulbs.co.uk) which has delicately swept-back petals of the purest white, mixed with the elegantly lily-shaped blooms of tulip.

Rivers of white daffodils and tulip bulbs will pop their pale, cheery heads up next spring if you plant them in November.

THREE OF THE BEST WHITE WINTER BLOOMS

Clematis 'Winter Beauty'
Come December-February, expect tumbling bell-shaped blooms from this climber. £19.99 crocus.co.uk

Christmas Rose
Bowl-shaped flowers stand in brilliant contrast against dark green leaves. £6.99 rhsplants.co.uk

Honeysuckle 'Winter Beauty'
Clusters of white blooms cling to bare branches December-March. £17.99 waitrosegarden.com

All is bright

Enjoy the calming glow of a candle and fill your house with the wonderful smells of the season with these handmade candles

rosemary & mandarin

hand poured, all natural

soy candle

Materials:

Soya wax flakes
Candle fragrance oils
Candle dye
Double boiler pan
Wooden lollipop sticks
Glass candle holder
Pre-made wicks or wicks
with sustainers for
soya wax
Cooking thermometer

1 Create the candle's wick by threading the waxed thread (or pre-made wicks) through the candle wick base and secure to the bottom of the glass candle holder using a dot of glue. Wrap the end of the waxed thread around a wooden lollipop stick so the wick is tight and stands upright in the candle holder.

2 Using a double boiler pan, pour water into the bottom, and soya wax pellets into the top. Melt until the wax is at a temperature of around 80°C.

3 Then add a small amount of the candle dye – ¼ tsp to ½ tsp depending on how vibrant you'd like it – and mix thoroughly. Add ½ tsp to 1 tsp of your chosen candle fragrance and mix thoroughly again.

4 Once the wax has cooled to 50-60 degrees Celsius pour the mixture into the glass candle holder, making sure the lollipop stick stays in the centre so the wick keeps straight as the candle sets

5 Leave the candle on a cooling rack for 24 hours, then cut off the excess wick leaving approximately 1cm of wick above the top of the candle. Decorate the candle with a label or hessian string tied in a bow. Then simply light, relax and enjoy.

Notable dates 2021

New Year's Day (Bank Holiday observed)	Friday January 1
Bank Holiday (Scotland)	Monday January 4
Epiphany	Wednesday January 6
Burns Night	Monday January 25
Chinese New Year (Ox)	Friday February 12
Valentine's Day	Sunday February 14
Shrove Tuesday	Tuesday February 16
Ash Wednesday	Wednesday February 17
St David's Day	Monday March 1
Commonwealth Day	Monday March 8
Mothering Sunday	Sunday March 14
St Patrick's Day	Wednesday March 17
First day of Passover (Jewish Holiday)	Saturday March 27
British Summer Time begins (clocks forward)	Sunday March 28
Palm Sunday	Sunday March 28
Maundy Thursday	Thursday April 1
Good Friday (Bank Holiday)	Friday April 2
Easter Sunday	Sunday April 4
Easter Monday (Bank Holiday)	Monday April 5
First day of Ramadan (Islam)	Monday April 12
St George's Day	Friday April 23
May Bank Holiday	Monday May 3
Ascension Day	Thursday May 13
Pentecost	Sunday May 23
Whit Monday	Monday May 24
Spring Bank Holiday	Monday May 31
Queen's Birthday	Saturday June 12
Father's Day	Sunday June 20
Summer Solstice (Longest day)	Monday June 21
Battle of the Boyne (Holiday N. Ireland)	Monday July 12
Summer Bank Holiday (Scotland)	Monday August 2
Summer Bank Holiday	Monday August 30
British Summer Time ends (clocks go back)	Sunday October 31
Hallowe'en	Sunday October 31
All Saints' Day	Monday November 1
Diwali (Hindu Festival)	Thursday November 4
Guy Fawkes Day	Friday November 5
Remembrance Sunday	Sunday November 14
First Sunday in advent	Sunday November 28
First day of Hanukkah (Jewish Holiday)	Sunday November 28
St Andrew's Day	Tuesday November 30
Winter Solstice (Shortest day)	Tuesday December 21
Christmas Eve	Friday December 24
Christmas Day	Saturday December 25
Boxing Day	Sunday December 26
Substitute Bank Holiday for Christmas Day	Monday December 27
Substitute Bank Holiday for Boxing Day	Tuesday December 28
New Year's Eve	Friday December 31

THE YEAR AHEAD

27 SUNDAY

28 MONDAY

29 TUESDAY

30 WEDNESDAY

31 THURSDAY

1 FRIDAY

2 SATURDAY

A magical memory

MY WONDERFUL WELSH MUM

My mother was incredibly beautiful – she had black hair and gimlet green eyes like a cat. Shortly before her 15th birthday, she came to London from Merthyr Tydfil in Wales to go into service in the East End of London. Despite only having a basic education, she could recite poetry off by heart – her favourite was The Wreck of the Hesperus by Henry Wadsworth Longfellow. She could also sing anything, from Madame Butterfly to traditional Welsh songs such as Myfanwy.

What's more, she was fun. She would always be out in the street turning the skipping rope for the children or playing hopscotch, laughing that infectious laugh I loved. Her capacity for hard work was unbelievable. She wasn't keen on cooking, but the house was polished to within an inch of its life. An accomplished needlewoman, she made sure every new baby in the neighbourhood had a finely crocheted shawl.

My mother was charitable to anyone who was down on their luck but didn't suffer fools gladly. Her sayings still run through my life – my favourite is "God liked common people, that's why he made so many of them".
Gwyneth M Lowe, Brentwood

Who am I?

I'm an actor born Christmas Day, 1899, best known for visiting a port in Morocco. I was the only member of cast on The African Queen not to contract dysentery from the water. The reason? I only drank whisky.

Humphrey Bogart

Nature diary

Replant a Christmas tree

No need to recycle a real Christmas tree, simply replant it in your garden and use it again next year. Choose a large plant pot with plenty of growing room and place in a cool, sheltered spot, watering and pruning regularly.

Make life easy

In need of a wardrobe clear out but can't decide what to get rid of? Find out what gets worn by hanging all your clothes facing to the back of the wardrobe. After you wear something put it back in with the hanger facing forwards. In six months have another look - you'll be able to see the items you don't wear. Easy!

Quirky Britain

The Tower of London's history as a menagerie dates back to the 13th Century when King John began using it to house his collection of wild animals. Thankfully, the only animals that inhabit the Royal Palace today are wire sculptured ones in the form of lions, monkeys, an elephant and a polar bear.

Recipe of the week

WINTER STEW OF CELERY, CHORIZO AND CANNELLINI BEANS

SERVES: 4-6
PREP: 15 MINS, PLUS SOAKING THE BEANS OVERNIGHT
COOK: 1 HOUR 30 MINS

2 tbsp olive oil
6 shallots, sliced
250g (9oz) chorizo, cut into 2cm slices
2-3 cloves garlic, crushed
1 tsp smoked paprika
½ head celery, each stalk cut into 3, plus leaves for garnish
1.5 litres (2.5pt) chicken or vegetable stock
500g (1lb 2oz) dried cannellini beans, soaked overnight in cold water
2 bay leaves
Salt and black pepper
Small bunch flat-leaf parsley, roughly chopped

1 Heat the oil in a large saucepan and sweat the shallots until soft and translucent, but not coloured.
2 Add the chorizo, turn up the heat slightly and continue frying until the chorizo and shallots are lightly caramelised.
3 Add the garlic, smoked paprika and celery and fry for a minute before pouring in stock.
4 Add the drained beans and bay leaves. Bring to the boil and simmer until beans are soft and tender (will take 1-1.5 hrs depending on the beans). Keep an eye on it and add a little cold water if it looks dry.
5 When the beans are cooked, stir through the parsley and season to taste. Serve scattered with the celery leaves.
www.lovecelery.co.uk

3 SUNDAY

4 MONDAY

5 TUESDAY

6 WEDNESDAY

7 THURSDAY

8 FRIDAY

9 SATURDAY

A magical memory

WALKING BACK TO HAPPINESS

Here I am coming out of the health centre in Greenford, Middlesex. I'm looking pleased with myself because it was my 'signing off' day. I had been born prematurely and had a few health problems – nothing major, but it was a worrying time for my mum and dad. On our regular visits to the clinic they were told that I would have difficulty walking as I didn't have a bone in the middle toe of each foot.

Of course I didn't know anything about this condition. The clinic advised that I should have braces made for my feet to help me walk. Mum was upset and Dad didn't think it was the right thing to do, but they went along with the suggestion. The braces arrived and I tried them on. They were large and clumsy and not at all comfortable. I had a few tears and Dad said that no way was I going to wear them.

By the time I was three and a half I could walk perfectly normally. As the picture shows, I was happy to be walking home, feeling very smart in my red coat, red hat and handbag (all made by Mum).
June Jones, Ringwood

Who am I?

I made my name getting an education in a 1983 play that later became a film, also starring Michael Caine. I then got my leggings on for a dance film, before taking a much-loved part in the Paddington movies.

Julie Walters

Nature diary

Snowdrop surprises

Look out for the first flowerings of snowdrops that usually raise their drowsy little heads between now and the middle of February. If you don't have any in your garden but want some for next spring, plant in March or April.

Make life easy

Doing a spot of decorating? Wrap a large elastic band around your paint pot from top to bottom and use it to wipe excess paint off your brush. In between coats wrap your brushes and rollers with either cling film or a plastic bag, to stop them drying out.

Quirky Britain

Be both amazed and amused at **House of Marbles** - an historic pottery-making site in Devon, dedicated to the production of marbles and other classic childhood pastimes. You'll find rooms filled with toys and games, ceramics, glassware and of course, marbles - not to mention lots of interesting hidden amusements along the way.

Recipe of the week

ALL-THE-GREENS RISOTTO

SERVES: 2 PREP: 5 MINS COOK: 25 MINS

1½ tbsp olive oil, plus extra for drizzling
80g (3oz) leek, diced
1 vegetable stock cube with 500ml (1pt) boiling water
2 cloves garlic, crushed
200g (7oz) risotto rice
1 courgette, coarsely grated
150g (5oz) cavolo nero, leaves left whole or finely sliced
50g (2oz) grated vegetarian hard cheese or parmesan
50g (2oz) unsalted butter

1 Heat 1 tbsp of olive oil in a wide pan over a medium heat.
2 Gently cook the leek for around 5 mins, stirring occasionally.
3 Make the stock.
4 Add the garlic and risotto rice to the pan and heat through, stirring continuously for 1 minute.
5 Add half the stock, stir thoroughly. Set a timer for 15 mins (or for the recommended rice cooking time minus 2 mins). Stir the rice continuously.
6 Cook the courgette separately in the remaining olive oil, add to the risotto pan when the timer says 10 mins.
7 Keep adding the stock a little at a time whenever the rice gets dry.
8 Add the cavolo nero when the timer shows 5 mins to go.
9 After 15 mins check the risotto is al dente.
10 Add the butter and some of the cheese (save a little for serving), stirring in gently until creamy.
11 Serve immediately, adding a sprinkling of cheese and a final drizzle of olive oil.
www.discovergreatveg.co.uk

10 SUNDAY

11 MONDAY

12 TUESDAY

13 WEDNESDAY

14 THURSDAY

15 FRIDAY

16 SATURDAY

A magical memory

GRANDMA'S CORNER SHOP

This picture shows the extension built onto our family home. It was originally run as a corner shop by my grandmother, Ellen, and later converted into a bedroom for my parents.

Separated from the kitchen by a doorway hung with blackout material left over from the war, the shop sold everyday items ranging from bread and tinned food to cigarettes and soap powder. The till was an old Oxo cube tin which was kept in a desk along with a book recording the purchases of customers on credit. The credit customers were local families with numerous children who lived 'on tick', buying their groceries on a promise to settle their accounts at the end of the week on payday. When the time came, they were often only able to pay part of what they owed. Without Ellen's tolerance of their situation, there would have been many a hungry child in the village.

We had a guard dog who was a useful deterrent against the local lads who thought they could make a few easy coppers by stealing returned lemonade bottles that were stored round the back of the shop and cheekily claiming the deposit on the 'empties'.
Margaret Campbell, Bathgate

Who am I?

Introduced to humanitarian work by Audrey Hepburn and a UNICEF Goodwill Ambassador for many years, most people consider me a saint. I have gone in reverse 700 times but my motto has always been to live and let die.

Roger Moore

Nature diary

Hunt under the hedgerows

Go exploring and gently peek under the hedgerows near you. Its residents, including hedgehogs and dormice, can be found snoozing in these areas during the chilly hibernation period. You may also see seven-spotted ladybirds huddled together to keep warm!

Make life easy

Clean dusty and hard-to-clean Venetian blinds with a pair of kitchen tongs. Simply wrap a microfibre cloth around each tong end and secure with an elastic band or hair bobble. Then spray the cloth with furniture polish or vinegar and slide your clever new cleaning tool through the gaps.

Quirky Britain

Visit **Whittlesey** in Cambridgeshire this January to witness the annual Straw Bear Festival. The event dates back more than 200 years and sees a performer wearing a five-stone metal and straw bear costume parading through the town streets with a troupe of Appalachian and Morris dancers. Its exact origins remain unknown.

Recipe of the week

CARAMEL LATTE SEEDED FLAPJACKS

SERVES: 16 PREP: 15 MINS COOK: 25 MINS

330ml carton of Arctic Iced Coffee Latte
150g (5oz) salted butter
55g (2oz) soft dark brown sugar
1tbsp golden syrup
250g (9oz) porridge oats
300g (10½oz) dried dates and apricots, chopped
100g (3½oz) mixed seeds
Melted chocolate (optional)

1 Preheat the oven to 180°C/350°F/Gas Mark 4.
2 Line a baking dish, approximately 25cm x 20cm with greaseproof paper.
3 In a saucepan bring the Arctic Iced Coffee to the boil until it reduces by around half the volume. Then turn down the heat and add the butter, sugar and syrup to the pan. Stir until the butter and sugar are melted and all is combined.
4 In a bowl, mix the oats, fruit and seeds then stir in the coffee mixture.
5 Tip into the prepared baking dish, spread evenly and bake for 25 mins until firm and golden.
6 Leave to cool in the dish then refrigerate.
7 Cut into 16 bars and drizzle with melted chocolate if desired.

www.arcticicedcoffee.co.uk

17 SUNDAY

18 MONDAY

19 TUESDAY

20 WEDNESDAY

21 THURSDAY

22 FRIDAY

23 SATURDAY

A magical memory

GOING THE EXTRA MILE

In the Forties I was a clerical assistant at a secondary modern school in New Romney in Kent. Part of the school was in a large old house and my office was little bigger than a cupboard, but it had a fireplace and in the winter the caretaker kept it well supplied with coal.

One of my jobs was to check the crates of milk delivered by the local dairy. When the bottles were covered with snow I could hardly feel my fingers. I took money to the bank once or twice a week and while I was out I called on local tradesmen to ask if they would like to advertise in the school magazine.

When the headmaster's wife returned to teaching after giving birth to a baby girl, the toddler was deposited in the office for me to look after. I used to take her with me in the pram when I did the banking. Occasionally I supervised the detention class while the teacher in charge went out for a smoke! None of this was in my job description, but I liked my work for which I was paid £52 a year plus a war bonus.
Ruth Spencer, Maidstone

Who am I?

I had the No 1 hit of 1967, which was also the name of a Sidney Poitier movie I appeared in. Later working with Take That and singing a Bond theme tune, my stardom led me to marry a Bee Gee.

Lulu

Nature diary

Sow sweet peas

Planting your sweet peas in winter makes for a more robust and stronger plant and gives you something colourful to look forward to come spring. Plant in a sunny position in well-drained soil or grow in a pot of peat-free compost.

Make life easy

Struggling to juice a really hard lemon? Pop it in the microwave for 7-10 seconds then roll it back and forth with your palm on your kitchen worktop. You'll then be able to squeeze out lots more juice. It works with other citrus fruits such as limes too!

Quirky Britain

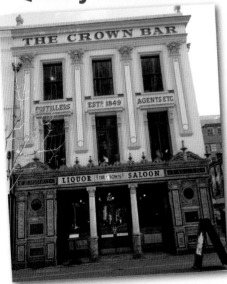

The Crown Liquor Saloon – a Victorian-era gem of a pub in Belfast – has been completely restored and preserved to its original state. A stunning example of a once hugely popular traditional Victorian gin palace, with original gaslighting, inside you'll find private booths, heated footrests at the bar and intricate mosaic tile flooring.

Recipe of the week

MUSHROOM AND GORGONZOLA OMELETTE

SERVES: 1 PREP: 10 MINS COOK: 10 MINS

2 tbsp butter
30g (1oz) mushrooms, roughly chopped
Salt and pepper
3 medium British Lion eggs
1 tbsp double cream
30g (1oz) gorgonzola, cut to small pieces
20g (¾oz) walnuts, roughly chopped
5g chives, chopped

1 Heat 1 tbsp butter in a small frying pan over a medium heat. Add the mushrooms and cook for 2-3 mins, until browned. Season generously with salt and pepper. Take off the heat and set aside.
2 In a small mixing bowl, whisk together the eggs and the double cream. Heat up the remaining tablespoon of butter in a small frying pan over a low heat. Add the whisked eggs and stir rapidly with a spatula for 1 min. Put a lid on and cook for another 1-2 mins.
3 When the base of your omelette is set, spread the gorgonzola cheese, mushrooms and walnuts over half of it. Fold the side without topping over the other and cook for 1-2 mins, until the cheese is melted and the eggs just slightly runny inside.
4 Sprinkle the omelette with chives and serve.

British Lion Eggs www.eggrecipes.co.uk

24 SUNDAY

25 MONDAY

26 TUESDAY

27 WEDNESDAY

28 THURSDAY

29 FRIDAY

30 SATURDAY

A magical memory

A GUINNESS AND A SING-SONG

As my father was in the army, I was born in Madras in India, but this photo of me with my parents-in-law was taken by a street photographer in London. I was staying with them while my husband Stan was away on National Service. We lived in Dunstable, but Dad was born in the East End and loved to go down there on a Sunday to meet up with his friends and have a pint or two. Mum liked to have a Guinness and a sing-song, too.

During the war, Stan and his brother John had been evacuated to a home in Northampton where they were not at all happy. To escape, they got on a train and hid when the ticket collector came round. They arrived in London during a bombing raid so they were unable to find their mum and dad who were in a shelter at the time. Luckily, a friend spotted them and said to Dad: "I thought you told me your boys were away in the country?" so the family was happily reunited for the rest of the war.
Mary Hicks, Dunstable

Who am I?

A book lover and a 'grate' Hollywood icon, I was the blonde bombshell. Perhaps my most famous role saw me sidle up to two cross-dressing musicians, or maybe you've seen me serenading someone special in a big white building.

Marilyn Monroe

Nature diary

The whole of the moon

There's something incredible about seeing a full moon in the sky. Head outside with a blanket and a flask on January 28 at around 7.15pm and keep an eye out for a wonderfully bright and clear full moon.

Make life easy

If your iron is leaving behind chalky marks, the problem is likely a build-up of limescale. Most irons have a cleaning function, but if not, de-scale yours by filling the reservoir with one-part vinegar and one-part water. Turn it on to a medium heat, then continually steam until empty. Rinse thoroughly.

Quirky Britain

Winged helmets, fur-trimmed tunics, flaming torches and rousing music – the people of Shetland know how to throw a party. **Up Helly Aa** is a 24-hour celebration of the island's Viking roots where costumed men stride through the streets to set fire to a longboat. This year, the fire festive falls on January 26.

Recipe of the week

VEGETABLE AND WALNUT RAGU

SERVES: 4 PREP: 15 MINS COOK: 40 MINS

1 tbsp oil
400g (14oz) sweet potatoes, peeled and diced
1 onion, chopped
1 red pepper, diced
100ml (4fl oz) red wine
50g (2oz) sun-dried tomato paste
250g (9oz) cherry tomatoes, halved
400g (14oz) can chopped tomatoes
100g (3½oz) California Walnut Halves
250ml (½pt) vegetable stock
1 courgette, diced
Salt and pepper
25g (1oz) basil, shredded
To serve: Cooked spaghetti and grated Parmigiano Reggiano

1 Heat the oil in a large saucepan and fry the sweet potatoes, onion and pepper for 5 mins. Add the wine and reduce by half.
2 Stir in the remaining ingredients (except the courgette and basil) and bring to the boil, cover and cook for 15 mins.
3 Add the courgette, simmer for 20 mins until the sauce has reduced, season to taste and stir in the basil.
4 Serve with cooked spaghetti and grated cheese.

www.californiawalnuts.co.uk

31 SUNDAY

1 MONDAY

2 TUESDAY

3 WEDNESDAY

4 THURSDAY

5 FRIDAY

6 SATURDAY

A magical memory

I WAS A SATURDAY GIRL

This is a photo of me (on the right) with a lady called Connie Pacey. It was taken on her 100th birthday. In the Seventies I worked as a Saturday girl in the jeweller's shop she owned with her husband, Mick, in Ealing. My duties, apart from serving customers and answering the phone, were stamping the shop's contact details on the small brown envelopes used for repairs, writing the prices on tiny white tags, polishing goods and checking the stock. They paid me £1 a day which was above the going rate.

As the premises were small, we had no 'facilities' of our own so by special arrangement we were allowed to use the toilets in the ABC cinema next door.

One day I was sent to collect some goods from a place in Hatton Garden. It was quite a long way from Ealing so I was given exact details of the route I was to take. When I returned safely and handed the items over, I was told they were worth £1,000 which was a huge sum in those days. I was pleased I hadn't known their value beforehand!
Linda Mundy via email

Who am I?

What a way to make a living! Songwriter, record producer, actress, businesswoman and humanitarian, I'm most passionate about getting children into reading. You could say I've been a busy lady since breaking into the country music scene in 1967.

Dolly Parton

Nature diary

Song thrush sings

Listen out for the tunes of one of nature's leading singers. This lovely little garden bird that's brown on top with a white belly covered in black, drop-shaped spots, normally starts practising its loud and repetitious songs from about now.

Make life easy

Put too much salt in while cooking? Try adding a teaspoon of honey or a squeeze of lemon. Both sweet and acidic flavours can help balance the salt overload. Adding extra water, wine or cream are other options for diluting the taste to save your culinary creations from disaster.

Quirky Britain

Visit three unusual museums for the price of one at **Cuckooland, Tabley, Cheshire**. Here you'll find a huge collection of more than 600 clocks on display, which were all made in the Black Forest region of Germany. Other things to see include a Vintage Motorcycle Collection, plus a collection of tools and machines.

Recipe of the week

BEETROOT, BROCCOLI, SMOKED CHEDDAR AND MUSTARD TART

SERVES: 8 PREP: 30 MINS, PLUS CHILL TIME
COOK: 1 HOUR 25 MINS

75g (3oz) blanched almonds
225g (8oz) plain flour, plus extra for dusting
130g (4½oz) chilled butter, cubed
Pinch of salt
1 large egg yolk
3-4 tbsp ice-cold water
100g (3½oz) Tenderstem broccoli
5 eggs
300ml (10fl oz) double cream
10 sprigs of thyme, leaves picked
125g (4½oz) smoked cheddar, grated
3 cooked whole beetroot, quartered

1 Preheat the oven to 180°C/350°F/Gas Mark 4.
2 Scatter the almonds in an oven tray and roast for 8 mins until golden. Set aside. Once cool tip into a food processor and blitz to fine crumbs.
3 Add the flour, butter and pinch of salt to the food processor and pulse until mixture resembles breadcrumbs. Add the egg yolk and blitz again, adding 1 tbsp chilled water at a time until the mixture comes together. Shape into a ball, wrap in cling film and refrigerate for 15 mins.
4 Flour work surface and roll pastry to a 0.5cm thickness. Transfer pastry to a 21cm x 5cm deep loose-bottomed round tin. Chill for 30 mins.
6 Prick the base with a fork. Line the pastry case with baking parchment and baking beans and bake for 25 mins. Remove paper and beans and return to the oven for 10 mins, until the pastry is golden and firm.
6 Blanch the broccoli in a pan of salted boiling water for 1 minute.
7 Whisk the eggs, then beat in the cream, thyme and cheese.
8 Pour the cream mixture into the tart case and add broccoli and beetroot. Bake for 40-50 mins until golden and set. Cool before releasing from the tin.
www.lovebeets.co.uk

7 SUNDAY

8 MONDAY

9 TUESDAY

10 WEDNESDAY

11 THURSDAY

12 FRIDAY

13 SATURDAY

A magical memory

MY BRAVE UNCLE BERT

My Uncle Bert was a war hero, but I didn't know that until I was grown up and came across this marvellous picture of him (centre) and his family when he was awarded the Distinguished Conduct Medal in 1945.

Born in 1920 in the village of Cwm, South Wales, Bert worked in the local coal mine before he joined the third battalion Monmouthshire Regiment. In 1940 he was posted to Londonderry in Northern Ireland where he met his future wife, Maureen (on the left in the photo).

Promoted to sergeant, in June 1944 he took part in the Normandy landings and a month later was badly wounded in action. Under heavy mortar fire, with all his officers either killed or wounded, Bert reorganised the platoon and carried on fighting until they had achieved their objective.

As a result of his wounds, Bert lost the lower part of his leg and had an artificial limb. Despite this, he won many walking races in later years and enjoyed his hobby of greyhound racing. Although the family settled in Ireland, I am still in touch with Bert's son, Brendan, who is the little boy holding his parents' hands.
Howard Robinson, Ebbw Vale

Who am I?

When I served in the forces, I created a magic comedy act. Then just like that, I was a star, headlining every variety show. Best known for my failed magic and iconic headwear, I died doing what I loved.

Tommy Cooper

Nature diary

Froggy findings

This is peak frog-breeding time so expect great bubbling jellies of frog spawn in garden ponds around this week. If you have a pond, don't be tempted to introduce frog spawn from elsewhere. Instead wait for frogs to find your pond and create their own.

Make life easy

Clear out a blocked drain by adding one-part bicarbonate of soda to one-part vinegar and swilling this mixture down the plug hole. Cover the plug hole with a damp cloth for five mins, then run plenty of hot water down the drain to clear out the blockage.

Quirky Britain

Glasgow's Mural Trail features a vibrant and diverse range of outdoor artwork with something to suit all tastes – from the beautiful and bright to the quirky and bizarre – all set within an easily walkable radius in the city centre. Highlights include depictions of wildlife, sportspeople and portraits Sir Billy Connolly.

Recipe of the week

COURGETTE, SWEETCORN HASH AND EGG FRY UP

SERVES: 2 PREP: 10 MINS COOK: 25 MINS

1 tbsp rapeseed oil
200g (7oz) potatoes, diced to 1.5-2cm cubes
Pinch of salt
1 garlic clove, peeled and sliced
1 shallot, peeled and finely sliced
1 small yellow courgette, turned into peels
200g (7oz) sweetcorn
15g (½oz) pine nuts
1 tsp chilli paste or Thai sriracha sauce
100ml (4fl oz) vegetable stock
20 cherry tomatoes, halved
2 medium British Lion eggs
10g (½oz) parsley, roughly chopped

1 Heat the oil in a frying pan over a medium heat. Add the diced potatoes and a pinch of salt. Cook for 5 mins, until the potatoes are browned. Add a splash of water and continue stirring for 3 mins.
2 Add the garlic, shallot, courgette, sweetcorn and pine nuts. Stir and cook for 3 mins. Add the chilli paste (or sriracha) with the stock. Leave to simmer for 5 mins until the water evaporates.
3 Add the cherry tomatoes and make two holes in the vegetable mix for the eggs. Add more oil if needed.
4 Crack the eggs into the holes. Cover with a lid and lower the heat. Cook for 3-5 mins until the egg whites are set.
5 Serve in the skillet with a sprinkle of parsley.

British Lion Eggs www.eggrecipes.co.uk

14 SUNDAY

15 MONDAY

16 TUESDAY

17 WEDNESDAY

18 THURSDAY

19 FRIDAY

20 SATURDAY

A magical memory

A COTTAGE IN THE COUNTRY

This photo of my grandparents was taken outside their cottage in a village just beyond Hereford in the Thirties. Standing behind them is my mother, Gladys, flanked by my uncles, Charles and Benjamin.

As a child, I loved staying with Granddad and Grandma Matthews even though their two-up, two-down cottage had no mod cons whatsoever. The only lighting was candles or gas lamps and water was collected from the village pump in a bucket. Washing in a tin bath in front of the range was all part of the novelty. En-suite washing facilities in the bedroom were a jug, a bowl and a gazunder which was emptied every morning into a bucket and taken to the toilet halfway down the back garden.

Food was kept in the walk-in larder on a slab of marble or in a wire-fronted cage. Everything was cooked on the kitchen range. At four o'clock every day, my 'chore' was to collect our milk from the farm. The farmer's wife always gave me a glass to drink. It was yummy, still warm from the cows – the milk we get today couldn't hold a candle to it.
Winifred Perrett, Salisbury

Who am I?

I first starred in the movie Gaslight before moving into musical theatre. Later in life you'd know me best for snooping around as the super-sleuth Jessica Fletcher or playing an adorable teapot in a Disney movie classic.

Angela Lansbury

Nature diary

Perfect pruning

Now is a great time to prune roses. Cut away any dead, diseased or damaged wood until it looks healthy with no brown in sight. With large-flowered roses, cut back the remaining healthy shoots to remove about half of their length.

Make life easy

Make fresh-cut flowers last longer with this bright idea. After cutting the stems at a 45° angle and removing any leaves below the water line, add fizzy lemonade to the water. The sugar and acid will help your blooms last longer. Some say adding a penny to the water can also help.

Quirky Britain

The ladies of **Olney in Buckinghamshire** mark Shrove Tuesday each year with a pancake race through the town. A tradition that dates back to 1445, the competitors must have lived in Olney for at least three months to compete. To take part they must wear a skirt, apron, cover their head and bring their own pancake!

Recipe of the week

PINK LADY APPLE AND RHUBARB TART

SERVES: 6-8 PREP: 45 MINS COOK: 35 MINS

300g (10½oz) rhubarb, roughly chopped
90g (3oz) sugar
2 tsp cornflour
2-3 Pink Lady apples
1 pack pre-rolled puff pastry
Egg wash

1 Make rhubarb purée by placing 200g (7oz) of the rhubarb, 60g (2oz) of the sugar and 3 tbsp of water in a saucepan. Cover with a lid and cook over a low heat until soft and falling apart. Cool then purée in a food processor. Return to saucepan, check sweetness and add more sugar if needed. Stir in 1½ tsp of cornflour and cook gently until thickened. Cool.
2 Preheat oven to 200°C/400°F/Gas Mark 6.
3 Cut apples into slices 2-3mm thick and cut out hearts. Unroll the puff pastry and place on baking tray. Gently score a border, approximately 1.5cm thick.
4 Spoon the cooled rhubarb purée onto the pastry, staying within the border. Top with the apple hearts.
5 Brush the border with egg wash. Sprinkle with sugar, if desired, and place in oven for 30-35 mins until the pastry is browned.
6 Make the rhubarb glaze. Place the remaining rhubarb, 30g (1oz) of sugar and 2 tbsp water in a small saucepan. Cook over a low heat until the rhubarb is soft. Cool slightly, before tipping into a fine sieve above a bowl to collect the juice. Return juice to the saucepan, add ½ tsp of cornflour and cook until slightly thickened.
7 When the tart is baked, let it cool slightly and brush with the rhubarb glaze.

www.pinkladyapples.co.uk

21 SUNDAY

22 MONDAY

23 TUESDAY

24 WEDNESDAY

25 THURSDAY

26 FRIDAY

27 SATURDAY

A magical memory

OVERCOMING ADVERSITY

I have always loved art, designing and needlework. Stitched on to the cushion I am holding in the photo above are these words by the poet Algernon Swinburne, 'Blossom by blossom, the spring begins'. I chose the maxim to celebrate coming through a difficult time in my life.

A gas explosion in a neighbouring property had wrecked part of my house, leaving me and my family temporarily homeless. To make matters worse, my portfolio of 30 paintings and drawings for a postgraduate course in fine art and art history was totally ruined. I spent the next six months living out of a suitcase in hotels while dealing with builders and insurance companies. In the afternoons, while my small son slept, I sketched and painted to complete my portfolio and, thankfully, passed my exam.

Back in my own home at last, I started knitting again and after winning several design competitions, I was invited to become a knitwear designer - the career of my dreams. Like sunshine after spring rain, I realised good things can come out of adversity.

Charmaine Fletcher, Basildon

Who am I?

While studying at Cambridge University, I joined the university drama club where I met the likes of Emma Thompson and Stephen Fry. I love to play the piano, but you'll know me best for Blackadder and House.

Hugh Laurie

Nature diary

Bloom and grow

Give a well-established flower border some extra blooms at no extra cost. Divide perennials such as hardy geraniums which will have now formed new growth under last year's leaves. Dig up carefully, divide so each plant has 3-5 shoots and healthy roots, then replant.

Make life easy

Make light work of cleaning limescale off your shower head and taps with the help of white vinegar. Fill a plastic bag without holes with vinegar (freezer bags work well) and place it over your shower head or tap securing with an elastic band. Leave overnight for spotless results.

Quirky Britain

The Cinema Museum in Kent celebrates the thrill of the pre-digital days when 'going to the pictures' was a ticket to escapism. Packed with old cinema posters, cinema staff uniforms and antique cinema fixtures, settle back, relax and let the glamour and nostalgia draw you in.

Recipe of the week

ROASTED SALMON CHOWDER

SERVES: 6 PREP: 5 MINS COOK: 25 MINS

1.5 litres (2½pt) hot chicken stock
800g (1lb 8oz) floury potatoes, chopped
1 leek, thinly sliced
4 Waitrose lightly smoked salmon fillets
1 lemon, juiced
170ml (6fl oz) tub single cream
1 bunch of salad onions

1 Preheat the oven to 200°C/400°F/Gas Mark 6.
2 Pour the stock into a large pan. Add the potatoes and leek, bring to the boil and simmer for 20 mins, until softened.
3 Arrange the salmon fillets on a baking sheet. Pour the lemon juice over and roast for 15 mins until just cooked through.
4 Break the salmon into large flakes and stir into the soup along with the cream and chopped salad onions. Heat through gently and season.
5 Ladle into bowls and serve.

www.waitrose.com/recipe

28 SUNDAY

1 MONDAY

2 TUESDAY

3 WEDNESDAY

4 THURSDAY

5 FRIDAY

6 SATURDAY

A magical memory

WORKING ALL HOURS

Here I am with my hard-working mum, Queenie (on the left). In the Forties she took over a newspaper stall outside Sloane Square tube station in London. As we lived in Hanwell, West London, she had to get up at 3am to walk a mile to catch a trolleybus to Ealing Broadway from where she got a tube to Sloane Square.

My father made her newspaper stand out of wood. The top was hinged to protect her from bad weather as she wasn't allowed to shelter inside the station. He must have done a good job as the stand survived two decades of use.

After selling the morning papers, Mum was home again by 9am, but had to repeat the whole process for the evening editions. She did all this on top of running the home and bringing up three children. And there were no labour-saving devices such as washing machines and fridges in those days! It wasn't until I was married with children of my own that I realised how hard my mother had worked. I am shocked now at the very long hours she kept, but as children we just took it all for granted.
Deidre Jordan, Bideford

Who am I?

Having always been close to my brother, together we became one of the best-loved sibling acts, even though I insisted I was just a 'drummer who sang'. But just when it felt like we'd only just begun, sadly tragedy struck.

Karen Carpenter

Nature diary

Fabulous fruit

Get set for a summer of homegrown fruit by planting a berry bush now. Find a sunlit space, soak the roots in water for 30 mins then plant in a hole big enough for the roots. Add compost, mulch and water.

Make life easy

Banish stinky trainers and sweaty boots by combining half a cup of baking soda with five drops each of eucalyptus and tea-tree essential oils. Mix well and then sprinkle lightly into your smelly shoes and leave overnight for fresher footwear come the morning.

Quirky Britain

Founded in 1653, **Chetham Library** in Manchester is the oldest in Britain and home to manuscripts, ancient texts and more. It's located in an impressive sandstone building that dates back to 1421, and originally housed the priests of Manchester's Medieval Collegiate Church.

Recipe of the week

TOASTED GARLIC HUMMUS WITH RADISHES AND PITTA BREAD

SERVES: 4 PREP: 10 MINS COOK: 5 MINS

Hummus:
6 cloves of garlic, sliced
4 tbsp extra-virgin olive oil
400g (14oz) tinned chickpeas, drained
1 lemon zested and juiced
1 tbsp tahini
Salt and pepper
Accompaniments:
400g (14oz) mixed radishes cut in half
4 warmed pitta breads
Mixed olives

1 Place the garlic and olive oil into a medium-sized frying pan, heat gently until the garlic starts to turn a golden brown, remove from the heat and set aside.
2 Place all the hummus ingredients into a food processor, blend until smooth and season with salt and pepper.
3 Serve with radishes, warmed pittas and olives.
www.loveradish.co.uk

8 SUNDAY

9 MONDAY

10 TUESDAY

11 WEDNESDAY

12 THURSDAY

13 FRIDAY

14 SATURDAY

A magical memory

THE WEEKEND STARTED HERE...

When I was growing up in the Fifties, Friday night was bath night. With no bathroom, things were very different from today. First, a large zinc pail was placed in the sink and filled with water which was then emptied into the copper which had been carried into the kitchen.

Next, the gas underneath the copper was lit. This entailed crawling on hands and knees and much undecipherable muttering from my father. As soon as the water was steaming hot, the pail was filled once again and the water was tipped into the tin bath which had been carried from its place on a hook on the landing.

After a towel had been placed on the floor to catch the drips, I was afforded the luxury of being first in the bath. How I longed to have a long soak, but it was a quick scrub and then out before the water got too cold for my parents to use. After everyone had washed, there was the never-ending job of scooping out the bath water, cleaning, wiping it down and putting it away. This rigmarole took up the rest of the evening, but I was tucked up in bed by then.

Yvonne Moxley, Harpenden

Who am I?

In the public eye from age 11, MGM launched my career in 1943 alongside a very special dog. My big violet eyes were offset by the jewellery I loved to wear, most of which were gifts from my many husbands.

Elizabeth Taylor

Nature diary

Simply the nest

Watch out for some key British bird species setting up home this week including blackbirds, blue tits, great tits and rooks who will all be building nests. You can help by leaving out natural fabrics, such as straws, grasses and pet hair for their nest.

Make life easy

Clean your microwave with this clever tip. Half fill a microwavable jug with water. Halve a lemon, squeeze into the water and add to the jug. Add a few tablespoons of white vinegar and heat on full power for three minutes. Leave the door closed for another five, before wiping.

Quirky Britain

In the Forest of Dean near Coleford, **Puzzlewood** is an enchanting maze of pathways winding through deep gulleys of moss-covered rocks and the twisted roots of Yew trees. It has an atmosphere quite unlike any other woodland - much like the setting of a fantasy film, where fantastic creatures lurk around every corner.

Recipe of the week

PAPRIKA AND WALNUT SCRAMBLED EGG BAGEL

SERVES: 1 PREP: 5 MINS COOK: 2-3 MINS

1 bagel, halved
75g (3oz) baby spinach
½ tbsp oil
¼ tsp smoked paprika
25g (1oz) California Walnut Pieces, chopped
2 medium eggs, beaten
1 tbsp milk
Sprinkle of chopped chives to serve

1 Toast the bagel and set on a plate.
2 Meanwhile, place the spinach in a microwaveable bowl, cover with cling film and microwave on high for 1 minute or until just wilted.
3 Heat the oil, paprika and walnuts in a small saucepan until it just starts to sizzle, remove and set aside. Beat the eggs and milk together and season. Add the eggs to the pan and stir gently to scramble.
4 Place the spinach on top of the bagel and top with the eggs. Serve sprinkled with the reserved walnuts and chives.
www.californiawalnuts.co.uk

14 SUNDAY

15 MONDAY

16 TUESDAY

17 WEDNESDAY

18 THURSDAY

19 FRIDAY

20 SATURDAY

A magical memory

LIGHTING THE WAY

This is the story of how an article in **Yours** magazine brought me a new friend as well as an absorbing new hobby. Written by Lorna Hanwell, the article was about her mother's experience of being brought up in a lighthouse family. I wrote to tell Lorna how much I enjoyed it and shared a few memories of my own local lighthouse at the Point of Ayre. She replied that one of her mother's aunts was married to the keeper of that same lighthouse. Sadly, she had died in childbirth over a hundred years ago and was buried somewhere on the Isle of Man. I promised to find her aunt's grave and place a flower on it. My husband and I found the grave in the parish of Bride.

After that I became interested in lighthouse keeping which, since automation took place in the Eighties, has become an almost forgotten way of life. I have even joined the Association of Lighthouse Keepers which aims to preserve as many lighthouses as possible. I find it an exciting hobby and have learned a lot from numerous books, visits and the encouragement of like-minded people.
Margaret Dodd, Isle of Man

Who am I?

When I fell off my bike as a child, I didn't realise the buck teeth that resulted would become my trademark. Always full of happiness, I became famous for long shows and the little men who joined me on-stage.

Ken Dodd

Nature diary

Great garlic

Before bluebells come and steal the show, look out this week for wild garlic taking over the woodland floor. Around footpaths and clearings expect to catch its powerful odour before it shoots a cluster of tiny white flowers come April.

Make life easy

Struggling to find the end of your sewing thread? Spray the end of the thread with hairspray to make threading it through the eye of your needle much easier. If you don't have any hair spray in the house, a touch of nail polish will do the same job. Just remember to not lick the thread later.

Quirky Britain

Situated on the Isle of Portland in Dorset, **Tout Quarry Park** creates an enchanting labyrinth of sculptures set above stunning views over Chesil Beach. With artwork created by well-known and emerging artists, have fun navigating the maze of paths, boulders and mini valleys to find each work of art.

Recipe of the week

CHOCOLATE CAKE

SERVES: 8-12 PREP: 15 MINS COOK: 25-30 MINS

For the cake:
200g (7oz) butter
200g (7oz) caster sugar
4 eggs
3 tbsp cocoa
200g (7oz) Doves Farm Organic Self-Raising White Flour
3 tbsp milk
1 tsp vanilla extract
For the filling:
100g (3½oz) unsalted butter
150g (5oz) icing sugar
2 tbsp cocoa
For the icing:
50g (2oz) chocolate
25g (1oz) butter
1 tbsp golden syrup

1 Preheat the oven to 180°C/350°F/Gas Mark 4. Line two 20cm round cake tins with parchment.
2 Beat butter and caster sugar together until light and fluffy.
3 Beat in one egg followed by a spoon of cocoa. Continue adding and beating in the remaining eggs, adding a spoon of cocoa each time.
4 Sieve the flour into the bowl. Add the milk and vanilla and stir to create a batter.
5 Divide the mixture between the tins. Bake for 25-30 mins.
6 Leave the cakes to cool for 5 mins, before turning out onto a wire rack.
For the filling:
7 Put the butter into a bowl and beat until softened. Sift the icing sugar and cocoa into the bowl and mix. Spread over one cake layer, then place the other layer on top.
For the icing:
8 Put the chocolate and butter into a bowl and melt. Stir, allow the mixture to cool, then stir in the golden syrup. Pour over the top of the cake.
www.dovesfarm.co.uk

21 SUNDAY

22 MONDAY

23 TUESDAY

24 WEDNESDAY

25 THURSDAY

26 FRIDAY

27 SATURDAY

A magical memory

MY VERY BEST DRESS

Oh, how I wish I still had this dress now! It was nylon, royal blue with white spots, a ruffled yoke and hand-sewn buttonholes. My lovely mother made it for me. She was the cook at a manor house and sewed it late at night after she had finished preparing a seven-course meal for the gentry who lived there. I was immensely proud to wear it and didn't mind the faint smell of onions from the meal she'd been making as I loved her so much and knew how tired she must have been.

Aged 13, I wore the dress to sing a solo at the Whit Sunday service at our village church in Somerset. It was a particularly happy time as my father had just retired from the RAF after the war.

Later that year, when I was confirmed by the Bishop of Bath and Wells, I was proud to wear another dress that my mother made from a parachute that had been given to my father. I still have that dress, although it is a wee bit too small for me now!

Jeanne Hoare-Matthews, Weston-super-Mare

Who am I?

I hit the big-time playing Polly Browne in a West End musical before starring as a fastidiously tidy nanny, a nun with a rebellious streak and the Queen of Genovia. I also wrote a children's book with my daughter.

Julie Andrews

Nature diary

Hang up happiness

Celebrate the arrival of spring with a beautiful hanging basket. If you're using a plastic or rattan basket, use three central plants, three bright plants (such as pansies or geranium) and six trailing plants (we love trailing fuchsia or petunia).

Make life easy

Damp kitchen sponges can quickly harbour germs and make the room smell, but chucking them out is costly and bad for the environment. Replace less frequently by zapping your wet sponge in the microwave for one minute to effectively kill any germs.

Quirky Britain

Enter a labyrinth of wonderful winding passages at **Margate's Shell Grotto**. Its shiny walls intricately decorated with mosaics made from 4.6 million seashells depict imagery of animals, gods and goddesses and other designs. It was accidently discovered in 1835, but nobody can explain who built this amazing place, or why.

Recipe of the week

LAMB STEW

SERVES: 6 PREP: 20 MINS COOK: 3 HOURS 30 MINS

1kg boned leg of lamb, trimmed and cut into 2cm pieces
Pinch of flaked sea salt
Black pepper
2 tbsp plain flour
50g (2oz) butter
1 tbsp olive oil
2 cloves of garlic, peeled and chopped
2 sprigs of rosemary
2 tbsp sunflower oil
1 large onion, halved and sliced
2 medium carrots, peeled and roughly diced
½ medium swede, peeled and roughly diced
1 litre (1¾pt) vegetable or lamb stock
400g (14oz) tin chopped tomatoes
2 fresh bay leaves
2 tbsp roughly chopped flat leaf parsley

1 Preheat the oven to 160°C/320°F/Gas Mark 3.
2 Season the lamb with salt and pepper, then dust with flour. In a large frying pan over a high heat, combine the butter, olive oil, garlic and rosemary. Once the butter is bubbling, place the lamb into the pan to sear (do this in batches).
3 Keep turning until each piece of lamb is browned and sealed on all sides. Set the browned meat, garlic and rosemary to one side.
4 Heat the sunflower oil in a large casserole dish. Add the onion, carrots and swede. Cook for 10 mins until starting to caramelise. Add the stock, tomatoes and bay leaves. Simmer for 10 mins then add lamb, garlic and rosemary.
5 Cover with lid and cook in the oven for 3 hours. If the stew looks too wet at the end cook for an extra 30 mins. If it's dry add a little water. Remove the bay leaves and rosemary sprigs before serving with mashed potato.

The mymuybueno Cookbook by Justine Murphy

28 SUNDAY

29 MONDAY

30 TUESDAY

31 WEDNESDAY

1 THURSDAY

2 FRIDAY

3 SATURDAY

A magical memory

A GRAND DAY FOR A WEDDING

I was 17 and Eric was 20 when we were married on the same day as the Grand National in April 1955. While the photographs were being taken, my new father-in-law and the Roman Catholic priest who married us were in the church porch with a transistor radio, listening to the race. Both men jumped for joy when the winner was announced!

Money was scarce. My mother gave up smoking and saved threepenny bits in a sweet jar to help pay for the wedding. My dress was borrowed from a friend and I was the seventeenth bride to wear it. The agreement was that I would pay to have it dry cleaned before returning it to her for the next bride to wear.

After Eric and I returned from our honeymoon in Llangollen, we started saving my wages (£5 a week) in a shoebox until we had £150 deposit to put on a house costing £1,350. I have a vivid memory of buying new lampshades at Woolworth's and waiting excitedly for darkness to fall so we could switch the lights on and run outside to admire them!
Joan Goodman, The Wirral

Who am I?

I'm an actor and director who uses my profile to raise awareness of humanitarian suffering in the world. When not saving the planet, you'll see me in the Oceans series or on ER. I'm married to a beautiful barrister.

George Clooney

Nature diary

Boxing hares

Ding ding, round one! Watch out for hares taking part in their annual boxing championships to win a mate this week. The best time to see them is dawn and dusk in open fields, farmland and woodland edges.

Make life easy

Avoid mismatched bedding by folding your clean bedding sets and sheets and storing them inside the matching pillowcases. If you have a large collection of linens, keeping them all in sets makes bed-change day far easier and saves rummaging through your linen drawer for hours.

Quirky Britain

The Widow's Buns is a yearly tradition where sailors from the Royal Navy place a hot cross bun in a net that hangs above the bar at **The Widow's Son pub** in Bromley. The legend behind the ceremony tells the story of a sailor who promised his widowed mother that he'd return for Good Friday, but never did.

Recipe of the week

CADBURY CREME EGG AND BEETROOT BROWNIES

MAKES: 20 PREP: 20 MINS COOK: 30 MINS

225g (8oz) dark chocolate
150g 5oz) butter
225g (8oz) golden caster sugar
3 eggs
120g (4½oz) plain flour
200g (7oz) cooked beetroot, grated
3 Creme Eggs, cut into 20 pieces

1 Preheat oven to 180°C/350°F/ Gas Mark 4.
2 Butter and line a 20cm x 30cm baking tin, 3-4cm deep with baking parchment.
3 Place the chocolate and butter in a bowl and melt, either in the microwave or over a pan of simmering water. Stir until smooth, then set aside to cool.
4 Whisk together the sugar and eggs in a large mixing bowl until pale and thick.
5 Whisk the cooled chocolate and butter into the eggs, then gently fold in the flour and grated beetroot until evenly mixed. Pour into the baking tin.
6 Dot the Creme Egg pieces on top of the batter, spacing them so that each square of brownie has one.
7 Bake for 25-30 mins until the brownie is firm. Leave to cool for 10 mins, then place on a wire rack. Once completely cool cut into 20 pieces.
Cadbury Creme Egg Cookbook

4 SUNDAY

5 MONDAY

6 TUESDAY

7 WEDNESDAY

8 THURSDAY

9 FRIDAY

10 SATURDAY

A magical memory

DEVOTED SISTERS

This is my gran (on the left) with her sister, Vera. They lived in the same house in Portsmouth for 95 years. Other relatives also lived there; these included their other sister, Flo, and their aunt, known as Nana, who looked after them when they were little. Eventually, Nana died, Flo got married and Gran also got married and had two children. Aunt Vera didn't marry until she was in her 40s but sadly didn't have any children. That was a shame because she would have made a wonderful mother.

As I grew up, Gran and Auntie Vera were two very important ladies in my life. I visited them regularly and stayed with them in the school holidays when my mother was at work. They showered me with love. I'm sure I must have got under their feet, but they took me out every day. We went to the shops in the morning and in the afternoons we went to the park where Gramps played outdoor bowls.

When they were both widowed, they relied on each other more than ever. Aunt Vera died suddenly, aged 95, and Gran followed shortly after. I don't think she could see the point of living without her sister.
Christine Barrow, Plympton

Who am I?
I rose to prominence as a Shakespearean actor, but went on to star in costume dramas, swashbucklers and horror films. I played suave villains like Mr Murdstone but am best known for occupying 221B Baker Street in several Hollywood films.

Basil Rathbone

Nature diary

Ladybird, ladybird

Say hello to some new arrivals in the garden as ladybirds emerge into the sunshine to roam through new foliage. Although there are 46 different types of ladybird in the UK, the most common is the bright red seven-spotted ladybird.

Make life easy

Don't forget to wipe your garden secateurs with a disinfectant in between pruning diseased plants to avoid transmitting the disease to other parts of your garden. Certain diseases like box blight also require stringent measures such as preventing soil transferring between plants and disinfecting footwear after use.

Quirky Britain

Egg Rolling is a big Easter tradition in **Preston**, with a history of more than 150 years. Hundreds of beautifully decorated eggs are rolled down the hill on the hour at Avenham Park. The event is traditionally held on Easter Monday (April 5) and brings an eclectic mix of workshops, street theatre and live music.

Recipe of the week

SWEET AND SMOKY BEETROOT SHAKSHUKA

SERVES: 4 PREP: 15 MINS COOK: 40 MINS

For the dukkah:
25g (1oz) pine nuts
½ tsp fennel seeds
½ tsp cumin seeds
½ tsp coriander seeds
1 tbsp sesame seeds

For the shakshuka:
2 tbsp olive oil
1 large red onion, sliced
2 garlic cloves, diced
2 tbsp tomato puree
100g (3½oz) diced chorizo
2 x 400g (14oz) tins plum tomatoes
2 tsp paprika
400g (14oz) canned chickpeas, drained
1 x 180g pack Love Beets Sweet + Smoky Shredded Beetroot
4 eggs
1 tbsp chopped mint
1 tbsp chopped coriander
1 tbsp chopped dill
Flatbreads, to serve

1 Add the dukkah ingredients to a frying pan, set over a low-medium heat and toast until the nuts are golden and spices fragrant.
2 Add the oil to a large ovenproof shallow pan and set over a low-medium heat. Add the onion cook, for 10 mins stirring occasionally until soft. Add the garlic and tomato purée and cook for 2 mins.
3 Stir in the chorizo and cook for 5 mins, then add the paprika, tomatoes, beetroot, chickpeas and 200ml (7floz) water. Cover and simmer for 20 mins, stirring occasionally, until thickened.
4 Use the back of a spoon to make four wells in the mixture and crack an egg into each well. Cover with a lid and cook until the eggs are cooked.
5 Scatter over the herbs and dukkah. Serve with warm flatbreads.

www.lovebeets.co.uk

11 SUNDAY

12 MONDAY

13 TUESDAY

14 WEDNESDAY

15 THURSDAY

16 FRIDAY

17 SATURDAY

A magical memory

ALWAYS THE BRIDESMAID

At the tender age of eight, being asked to be a bridesmaid was an exciting privilege. The bride-to-be was Myrtle, the pretty girl who lived next door to us in Devon.

I was to be a princess for a day with new white shoes and a long pale blue dress which my mother would have made (I can still hear the clickety-clack of her hand-driven Singer sewing machine as I write.) I was fortunate to have naturally curly hair which I wore in plaits for school but on special occasions it was allowed to hang loose.

One of Myrtle's sisters, Rene, was the other bridesmaid and I think the lady to the left of the bride in the group photo was the matron of honour. When the day of the wedding finally arrived, we were driven to the church in a car and even that was a luxury in those days. The organ music rang out 'Here comes the bride' as we followed her down the aisle.

Over the years, I was asked to be a bridesmaid on another three occasions before I finally became a bride at my own wedding in 1959.
Sheila Mills, Minehead

Who am I?

After Bringing Up Baby with Cary Grant, I acquired the rights to The Philadelphia Story which I also starred in. In the Forties I started a screen and romantic partnership with Spencer Tracy, although I fiercely defended my private life.

Katharine Hepburn

Nature diary

Look after youngsters

Protect emerging seedlings from slugs and snails by mulching around the base of plants with horticultural grit which they find it hard to travel over. Also consider a beer trap where you half-fill a container in the ground with cheap beer which entices them in.

Make life easy

Keep bananas for longer by wrapping the stems in cling film. This slows the release of a gas called ethylene, which is what causes it to ripen in the first place. Storing your bananas with other fruit will also ripen them faster, so keep them separate.

Quirky Britain

Founded more than 800 years ago in 1152, **Kirkstall Abbey** boasts historic architecture amid a haven of wildlife and greenery and is one of the UK's most complete Cistercian monasteries. As well as exploring the ruins, visitors can let their imaginations be transported back in time at the interactive visitor centre.

Recipe of the week

VERY VEGGIE LASAGNE

SERVES: 4-6 PREP: 40 MINS COOK: 40 MINS

Tomato sauce:
2 tbsp olive oil
1 onion, chopped finely
1 carrot, chopped finely
2 celery sticks, chopped finely
2 garlic cloves, crushed
2 tsp dried Italian mixed herbs
600g (1lb 5oz) British classic tomatoes, roughly chopped
300ml (10fl oz) vegetable stock
Veg mixture:
500g (1lb 2oz) sweet potatoes, peeled and cut into 2cm chunks
1 red onion, cut into wedges
1 yellow or red pepper, deseeded and cut into chunks
1 courgette, cut into chunks
1 tbsp olive oil
Salt and black pepper
20 British cherry tomatoes, halved
1 red chilli, deseeded and thinly sliced
Cheese sauce:
450ml (15fl oz) milk
40g (1½oz) plain flour
30g (1oz) butter
125g (4½oz) mature Cheddar cheese, grated
6-8 lasagne sheets

1 Heat the olive oil in a saucepan. Fry the onion, carrot, celery and garlic for 8-10 mins, until soft. Add the herbs and tomatoes and fry for few mins. Add the vegetable stock. Simmer for 18-20 mins until reduced and thickened. Purée in a blender. Set aside.

2 Preheat the oven to 200°C/400°F/Gas Mark 6.

3 Add the sweet potatoes, red onion, pepper, courgette and olive oil to a large roasting tin. Season and roast for 25 mins until tender. Add tomatoes, chilli and stir in the tomato sauce.

4 Make the sauce. Add milk, flour and butter into a saucepan and heat, stirring until the sauce thickens. Remove from heat and stir in half the cheese. Season.

5 Tip half the vegetable mixture into a large rectangular baking dish. Arrange half the lasagne sheets on top, spread half the cheese sauce over. Repeat the layers. Sprinkle over the remaining cheese.

6 Bake for 35-40 mins, until golden brown.

British Tomato Grower's Association www.britishtomatoes.co.uk

18 SUNDAY

19 MONDAY

20 TUESDAY

21 WEDNESDAY

22 THURSDAY

23 FRIDAY

24 SATURDAY

A magical memory

MY OWN MOTHER TERESA

I was blessed with a very special, loving mother (on the right in our photo). Her name was Teresa and she was 18 when she married my dad. Their wedding photos show her to have been a beautiful slim bride with long curly black hair.

I was born when she was 21 and was cherished by both my parents. As an only child, I went everywhere with them, to church bazaars, concerts and plays. Mum even used to come and look through the school gates to check that I was alright! I don't think she trusted anyone else to look after me.

I was told that she tried to learn to drive but never took her test. Apparently, she used to drive through roundabouts instead of around them. On one occasion when she was riding pillion on Dad's motorbike she was left behind at the traffic lights because she stood up to stretch her legs and when the lights changed he set off without her!

Mum loved people of all ages and was especially good with children, making up stories and inventing simple games for them. She enjoyed parties, singing and cooking - her steak puddings and huge Cornish pasties were renowned.

Janet Dandy, Burnley

Who am I?

I've sold more than 80 million records worldwide and with bandmate Dave Stewart. I've worked tirelessly for Greenpeace, Amnesty International and Nelson Mandela's 46664 Foundation. You'll hear me singing Here Comes the Rain Again and Love Song For a Vampire.

Annie Lennox

Nature diary

Earth day

April 22 marks Earth Day where people around the world can show their appreciation for our beautiful planet. A great way to mark this is to make one change, perhaps collecting rainwater in a bucket via a downpipe to water your plants.

Make life easy

Run out of glass cleaner? Make your own by combining a quarter cup of white vinegar, with two cups of warm water and a tablespoon of cornflour. Mix thoroughly and transfer to an empty spray bottle. Spray onto your windows and use with a clean cloth for sparkling results.

Quirky Britain

Love them or loathe them, there's no denying that gnomes are a British institution! See more than 1,000 in the woodlands at the enchanting four-acre **Gnome Reserve**, near Bradworthy in Devon - it's in the Guinness Book of World Records for the largest collection and includes lots of antique varieties.

Recipe of the week

CREAMY ASPARAGUS PASTA

SERVES: 4 PREP: 10 MINS COOK: 30 MINS

250g (9oz) pasta shapes
1 bunch asparagus, washed and trimmed
150g (5oz) frozen peas
1 tbsp olive oil
1 red onion, chopped
4 cloves garlic, crushed
1 tbsp plain flour
100ml (4fl oz) vegetable stock
200ml (7fl oz) milk
75g (3oz) cream cheese
3 tbsp Parmesan cheese
Salt and pepper
2 tbsp chopped flat-leaf parsley

1 Cook the pasta as per the instructions on the pack. In the last three minutes of cooking, add the asparagus and peas to pasta pot. Cook until pasta is al dente and vegetables cooked, then drain.
2 To make your sauce, heat the olive oil in a large pan over a medium heat. Cook the onion and garlic until soft, approximately five mins. In a bowl, combine the flour and stock and mix until smooth. Add to the onion mixture in the pan. Whisk in the milk and bring to a simmer. Stir in the cream cheese and Parmesan and season.
3 Stir the pasta and vegetables into the hot sauce and serve with the chopped parsley sprinkled over and a little extra Parmesan.
www.britishasparagus.com

25 SUNDAY

26 MONDAY

27 TUESDAY

28 WEDNESDAY

29 THURSDAY

30 FRIDAY

1 SATURDAY

A magical memory

WHERE'S LITTLE DAPHNE?

Here I am in my grandmother's garden holding a kitten called Smoky. My two sisters and I spent much of the war years evacuated with our grandmother in the beautiful little village of Partrington in the East Riding of Yorkshire. Wesley House, which had been the manse for the adjoining Methodist chapel, had six bedrooms, a large garden and a stable where we could play when it was wet.

On one particular day, I decided to hide from my little Welsh granny by staying in my bedroom playing with my doll, Betty. I could hear her asking my sisters where I was, but they didn't seem to know. Then I heard her, sounding very anxious indeed, calling over the wall to the next-door neighbour: "Mrs Howlet, have you seen Daphne? We can't find her anywhere."

That was when I realised that perhaps it wasn't very kind to worry Granny so much, so I picked Betty up and wandered downstairs. I was aged about seven but all these years later I can still recall feeling rather ashamed of myself when she and my sisters were so relieved to have found me.
Daphne Clarke, Richmond

Who am I?

Born in Bradford in 1929, I'm an actor, writer, critic and broadcaster, best known for my comedy sketch show with a man of the same first name that ran from 1971-1986 and my love of a certain breakfast item.

Ronnie Barker

Nature diary

Brilliant bats

It's time to keep your eyes peeled for bats in the night sky. After a period of hibernation they're now out in full force and especially hungry. They can be seen feeding most nights when it's not too wet or windy.

Make life easy

Coffee filters are far more useful than you might think. Handy for making glassware sparkle, use them to give smear-free results on your specs, windows, mirrors and computer screens. They're also perfect for lining plant pots to stop the soil from leaking out the hole in the bottom.

Quirky Britain

Situated in one of London's great green spaces, **the Dinosaur Trail at Crystal Palace** takes you past more than 30 sculptures of dinosaurs and other extinct animals. They were created in around 1854 and intended to be full-scale models of the prehistoric creatures, but are inaccurate based on what we know today.

Recipe of the week

GRILLED MACKEREL AND WATERCRESS SALAD WITH ORANGE AND CHILLI

SERVES: 2 PREP: 20 MINS COOK: 5 MINS

2 oranges
½ tsp ground coriander
½ tsp ground black pepper
1 red chilli, deseeded and finely chopped
4 mackerel fillets
½ tsp Dijon mustard
½ tbsp honey
85g (3oz) watercress
½ a small red onion, finely sliced

1 Preheat the grill to medium-high.
2 Zest half an orange and mix with the coriander, black pepper, and half the chopped chilli. Lightly score the skin of the mackerel fillets with a sharp knife. Press the spice mixture into the skin.
3 Segment the oranges. Cut off the top and bottom, cut away any peel and pith. Over a bowl, use a knife to cut each segment away from the centre. Put the segments to one side and squeeze the remaining orange to release any juice.
4 Measure 2 tbsp of the orange juice into a small bowl, then mix the with mustard, honey and remaining chopped chilli.
5 Place the mackerel fillet skin side up on a grill tray. Grill for 4-5 mins or until cooked through with crispy skin.
6 Divide the watercress between four plates. Scatter with the orange segments and red onion. Drizzle with the orange dressing and top with the mackerel.

www.watercress.co.uk

2 SUNDAY

3 MONDAY

4 TUESDAY

5 WEDNESDAY

6 THURSDAY

7 FRIDAY

8 SATURDAY

A magical memory

THE DAY PEACE BROKE OUT

When VE Day was declared on May 8, 1945, there were street parties and parades. We danced in barns, bus depots and even on the road in the moonlight! My resentment about being an evacuee faded and the air-raid shelter lost its horror. I dreamed of a brave new world and a bright future for my teenage years. The blackout curtains could go, food rationing would stop and glamorous clothes would be on sale without the need for coupons. No more torpedoes would be aimed at my dad's ship and my cousins would come home from prisoner-of-war camps. Church bells would ring on Sundays and there would be no more worries.

I couldn't remember men wearing civilian clothes or a beach without anti-tank blocks and barbed wire. I couldn't remember what a banana tasted like.

Football and other sporting activities returned to our lives. But as things turned out, food was still rationed and we still needed coupons to buy clothes when I got married years later in 1952. We had won the war, but I wondered if we had won the peace?
Pat Berkshire, Hexham

Who am I?

Having started my career in musical theatre, it was telly that made my name with a character whose delusions of grandeur and candlelight suppers delighted audiences in a hit BBC sitcom. I also appeared in Alan Bennett's Talking Heads.

Patricia Routledge

Nature diary

Go wild

Now's the perfect time to sow wild flower seeds to help provide nectar for insects such as bees, hoverflies and butterflies in the months to come. Annual wildflower seeds such as cornflowers, poppies and corncockle look lovely scattered in beds and borders.

Make life easy

Lost an earring back or other small item somewhere on the carpet? Wrap a sock or pair of tights around the end of your vacuum cleaner and secure with an elastic band. Use the nozzle to find the lost item without sucking it up and losing it in the vacuum.

Quirky Britain

A magical landscape of snail-shaped grass mounds, twisting DNA helix sculptures and artificial lakes make up **the Garden of Cosmic Speculation** - a 30-acre private garden near Dumfries in Scotland, whose design is inspired by modern cosmology. It's open just one day per year, typically the first Sunday of May.

Recipe of the week

BROCCOLI COUSCOUS PANCAKES

SERVES: 3 PREP: 15 MINS COOK: 15 MINS

150g (5oz) Tenderstem broccoli, plus 75g (3oz) extra boiled or steamed broccoli to serve
50g (2oz) raw couscous
80g (3oz) crumbled feta, plus extra to serve
1 clove garlic, finely chopped
3 sprigs mint, finely chopped
3 sprigs parsley, finely chopped
2 pinches dried chilli flakes
3 eggs, whisked
Salt and pepper
1-2 tbsp olive oil
2 tbsp low-fat plain yogurt (optional)

1 Blanch the broccoli in boiling salted water until bright green, drain and leave to cool. Once cooled blend in a food processor until finely chopped.
2 Add the couscous to a bowl and cover with 60ml (2floz) of boiling water. Cover with cling film for 5 mins until completely absorbed. Once cooked fluff up the couscous with a fork.
3 Add the broccoli, feta, garlic, mint, parsley, chilli, eggs, salt and pepper to the couscous and mix.
4 Heat a non-stick frying pan on a medium heat with some olive oil and spoon 1½ tbsp of the mix into the pan. Fry until golden brown on both sides.
5 Serve with a sprinkle of feta and broccoli on top or add a dollop of yogurt.

www.tenderstem.co.uk

9 SUNDAY

10 MONDAY

11 TUESDAY

12 WEDNESDAY

13 THURSDAY

14 FRIDAY

15 SATURDAY

A magical memory

A BIG-HEARTED LADY

My mum was an incredibly strong woman with the biggest heart in the world. She had a difficult childhood and her first husband was killed in the war. In the photo she is with her second husband, my father, who came from a well-off family. He was a lovely man but had no idea about money although he was good at spending it! It was Mum who kept our family together.

When we were in danger of being homeless, she walked the streets with the local paper until she found two rooms for us to live in. Despite the cramped conditions, she made it a home. We were able to move out when my sister got us a house through her job at The Co-op. As we all grew up, Mum was always there for us through life's ups and downs. She embraced our mixed-race family and supported me when I became a single mum.

After nursing my dad through dementia, she moved into sheltered accommodation where she made a point of befriending other residents who had no friends or relatives. She died at the age of 93 and we all miss her terribly.

Ann Rowe, Plumstead

Who am I?

Born of Italian immigrants, I grew up on the gritty streets of New York to become one of the founding fathers of the biggest swing group in history. You might have also seen me in From Here to Eternity.

Frank Sinatra

Nature diary

Good old gladioli

These beautiful flowers will bring colour to any garden this summer! Plant your bulbs in a sunny position with well-drained soil. Use a garden fork to dig over the planting area to a depth of 20-25cm and improve the soil with well-rotted compost to help hold plenty of moisture to ensure good quality blooms.

Make life easy

Run a stubborn jar lid under hot water to make it easier to undo. You could also try inserting a butter knife under the seal and levering it up slightly to help break the seal. Pop on a pair of rubber gloves to give more grip and the lid should easily twist off.

Quirky Britain

Every May through to September, **The Highland Games** are a kind of Scottish Olympics, where people compete in traditional Scottish sports. Most involve throwing heavy objects, including Tossing the Caber (throwing a huge wooden pole) and Hammer Throwing. Every Highland game event is unique and they are held across several stunning Scottish locations.

Recipe of the week

PINEAPPLE WHITE CHOCOLATE CAKE WITH SALTED BROWN SUGAR GLAZE

SERVES: 8 PREP: 10 MINS COOK: 40 MINS

200g (7oz) unsalted butter
200g (7oz) golden caster or granulated sugar
1 tsp vanilla extract
3 large eggs
200g (7oz) ground almonds
100g (3½oz) plain flour
1 tsp baking powder
100g (3½oz) white chocolate chips
1 x 435g tin Del Monte Pineapple Chunks in Juice, drained (reserve the juice)
A few sprigs of fresh thyme
Reserved tinned pineapple juice
2 tbsp light brown sugar
¼ tsp sea salt

1 Preheat the oven to 170°C/325°F/Gas Mark 3.
2 Line a round 20cm diameter loose-bottomed cake tin with baking parchment. Cut the butter into chunks and place in a large bowl with the sugar. Whisk until fluffy (3-4 mins).
3 Add the vanilla extract, whisk, then add the eggs one at a time. Fold in the ground almonds, flour and baking powder.
4 Stir in the chocolate chips then add to the cake tin. Level the mixture.
5 Arrange the pineapple chunks on top and push in slightly.
6 Bake for 35-40 mins – until an inserted skewer comes out clean. Leave to cool.
7 Make the sugar glaze. Pour the pineapple juice into a saucepan. Bring to the boil and simmer for 8-10 mins until reduced by half and slightly thickened. Add the brown sugar and stir until dissolved. Add the salt.
8 Cool to room temperature. Drizzle the sugar glaze over the cake. Arrange a few thyme sprigs on top, then serve.

Recipe from Nicky Corbishley for Del Monte UK

16 SUNDAY

17 MONDAY

18 TUESDAY

19 WEDNESDAY

20 THURSDAY

21 FRIDAY

22 SATURDAY

A magical memory

DAD AND HIS HOBBIES

On a walk around Emsworth, Hampshire, my father took this photo of me (on the left) with my mother and younger sister, Sandra. Photography was one of his many hobbies and when I was a teenager I would accompany him around our local town on Saturdays, my chief purpose being to carry the cameras. He photographed me, the pond, passers-by and anything that stood still for long enough. He had a special affinity with children, being much like a child himself.

After lunch at home, the morning's films would be developed. The larder doubled as the darkroom and we had strict instructions not to open the sitting room door which was next to it. One chink of light could ruin the film. Various stages followed, including developing. This involved lowering blank pieces of paper into a tray of fluid when, miraculously, a picture would appear. This was pegged on a line to dry, then the edges were trimmed with a guillotine that I was not allowed to touch.

Although he never lost his love of cameras, by the time I was 15, my father had moved on. His next craze was making ginger beer, but that's another story!
Wendy Chappell, Havant

Who am I?

Born in Morecombe, I made my name as a talking head, worrying about the cracker under the sofa, as well as my role in Last of the Summer Wine. I also made a cameo as Dolly's mum in Dinnerladies.

Thora Hird

Nature diary

Egg-cellent fertiliser

Don't throw away your eggshells as they make a great fertilliser. Leave out to dry fully before popping them into a blender and blitz them until they are powdery and fine. Sprinkle this powder around your garden plants.

Make life easy

Make an orange or lemon peel pot for seedlings. Halve your fruit and scoop out the insides. Add a small hole in the bottom for drainage, fill with soil and plant your seed. When your seedling is ready plant the whole thing into your garden where the peel will decompose.

Quirky Britain

The Cheese Rolling Championship is exactly what it sounds like – but with a bit of chasing involved. Every Spring Bank Holiday, people race down Cooper's Hill in the Cotswolds after a huge round of Double Gloucester cheese that travels up to 70mph. The winner is the first over the finishing line!

Recipe of the week

PARMA-WRAPPED FISH TRAY BAKE WITH VINE TOMATOES

SERVES: 4 PREP: 10 MINS COOK: 20 MINS

12 small peppers, halved
1 lemon, cut into wedges
2 tbsp olive oil
4 cod loin fillets (weighing about 150g (5oz) each)
8-12 basil leaves, plus extra to garnish
4 slices Parma ham
4 sprigs of British baby plum or cherry tomatoes on the vine
Salt and freshly ground black pepper

1 Preheat the oven to 200°C/400°F/Gas Mark 6.
2 Put the pepper halves and lemon wedges into a roasting dish. Drizzle with olive oil, season and then roast for 10 mins.
3 Meanwhile, arrange 2-3 basil leaves on top of each piece of cod, then wrap each fillet with a slice of Parma ham. Arrange on top of the peppers, then add the sprigs of tomatoes. Roast for a further 10-12 mins.
4 Serve garnished with extra basil leaves.

British Tomato Grower's Association www.britishtomatoes.co.uk

23 SUNDAY

24 MONDAY

25 TUESDAY

26 WEDNESDAY

27 THURSDAY

28 FRIDAY

29 SATURDAY

A magical memory

DANCE, LITTLE LADY, DANCE

This photo was taken for Picture Post magazine when I was working a summer season at the Pier Theatre in Eastbourne. I am on the right of comedian Sandy Powell, teaching him the steps.

Inspired by the child star Shirley Temple, I had wanted to dance from the age of three and a half. I will always be grateful to my mother who somehow found the money for me to attend dancing school for 11 years. Instead of going on to college from grammar school, I wanted to go on the stage. To attend the audition I had to have permission from the headmistress who did not approve and told me that going on the stage was not the thing for young ladies to do!

However, she did give in and I had a wonderful career that included being one of the Tiller girls at the London Palladium and a summer season at Blackpool's Opera House with such famous names as Harry Secombe, Eve Boswell and Val Doonican. After 21 years, I gave up touring to teach dance at adult education classes in London.

Barbie Carson, Warminster

Who am I?

Having grown up on music hall variety, I apparently became Charlie Chaplin's 'favourite clown', best known for slapstick films, mainly playing the hapless Norman Pitkin. In later life I turned serious for the TV adaptation of Going Gently. Norman Wisdom

Nature diary

Be a swift saviour

Look out early morning or dusk and chances are you might spot some newly arrived swift guests around. These birds are superb fliers but their numbers are plummeting. You can help by setting up a swift nest box on the outside of your home.

Make life easy

Make your own low-cost garden watering system using an old hose pipe. Drill evenly spaced small holes along a hose pipe length, being careful to only drill through one side. Attach a hose pipe cap to the end and position it around your flower beds to make a DIY sprinkler.

Quirky Britain

The annual **Maldon Mud Race** sees hundreds of competitors complete a 400-metre dash over the bed of the River Blackwater. The event can only take place when the water is low enough to allow participants to run safely through the water to the opposite bank and back again.

Recipe of the week

CAVOLO NERO SALAD WITH SWEET POTATO, PEAR, WALNUT AND BLUE CHEESE

SERVES: 2 PREP: 5 MINS COOK: 20 MINS

200g (7oz) sweet potato, chopped into 1cm cubes
1 tbsp olive oil
100g (3½oz) cavolo nero (Italian kale), sliced
1-2 ripe pears
50g (2oz) watercress
40g (1½oz) walnut pieces
50g (2oz) blue cheese (eg. Stilton)
Dressing:
3 tbsp olive oil
1 tbsp white wine vinegar
1 tsp clear honey
1 tsp wholegrain mustard

1 Preheat the oven to 180°C/350°F/Gas Mark 4.
2 Place the sweet potato cubes on a baking tray and drizzle with the olive oil. Bake for around 15 mins, until soft.
3 Meanwhile whisk together all the dressing ingredients and set aside.
4 Bring a small pan of water to the boil. Blanch the cavolo nero for 5 mins or until tender.
5 Quarter, core and thinly slice the pears. Mix the cavolo nero, watercress and pear slices in a bowl and stir in most of the dressing.
6 Toast the walnut pieces for 2 mins in a dry saucepan.
7 Add the walnuts and sweet potato to the bowl. Crumble the blue cheese on top and drizzle over the remaining dressing.
www.discovergreatveg.co.uk

30 SUNDAY

31 MONDAY

1 TUESDAY

2 WEDNESDAY

3 THURSDAY

4 FRIDAY

5 SATURDAY

A magical memory

A BUTLIN'S BEGINNER

Here I am, aged around four, with my mum and dad on my first ever holiday at Butlin's holiday camp in Ayr, Scotland. We are sitting on the wooden stairs leading to our chalet.

At that age, just climbing the ladder to sleep on the top bunk seemed like a great adventure. I remember playing on my scooter, making it go faster outside our row of chalets. I also loved the funfair, especially watching the candyfloss being spun in a steel container that went round and round.

Other novelties included going on the chair-o-planes and steering the tiny boats on the lake. Apparently, I gave everyone a fright when I jumped into the deep end of the swimming pool.

I was a shy little girl who always had a book in her hand. In the evenings, I would ready one of my Ladybird books. My favourite story was The Princess and the Pea – I wondered how she would have managed in my bunk bed.

I have to smile when I see that my socks are falling down and my new sandals are already scuffed. I've never been someone who can stay looking immaculate for long.

Sharon Haston via email

Who am I?

I played the ultimate top gun and completed the most impossible missions. My first leading role was in Risky Business in which I danced in my underwear, socks and shirt. I also played Claus von Stauffenberg and Ron Kovic.

Tom Cruise

Nature diary

Here be dragonflies

Listen out for the hum of a busy dragonfly doing the rounds this week. Some of the most common UK dragonflies include the bright green southern hawker and emperor with a sky blue or green abdomen. Attract dragonflies to your garden with a pond.

Make life easy

For a chemical-free way to clean your home try this simple recipe. Combine one-part white vinegar and one-part water, then add a herb of your choice to the mix. Sage and rosemary work well. Use as a general-purpose kitchen and bathroom cleaner that smells instantly and naturally fresh.

Quirky Britain

Celebrating the Cotswold village's wool-making past, the **Tetbury Woolsack Races** are a test of strength and fitness, as competitors carry a sack of wool up and down a steep hill. Held over the late May Bank Holiday each year, it sees men and women cover a course of 240 yards while carrying their woolsack.

Recipe of the week

CHORIZO, CHEESE AND WATERCRESS TOASTIE

SERVES: 4 PREP: 10 MINS COOK: 10 MINS

200g (7oz) cooking chorizo
Splash of olive oil
3 tbsp salted butter, softened
8 slices sourdough bread, not too thick
200g (7oz) gruyere, sliced
200g (7oz) sharp cheddar, sliced
½ a red onion, finely sliced
1 x 85g (3oz) bag watercress

1 Thickly slice the chorizo at an angle. Place a large frying pan over a high heat with a splash of olive oil. Fry the chorizo for a few minutes, turning frequently to prevent burning. Remove from the heat and drain the slices on kitchen paper.
2 Butter your bread slices (one side only). The buttered side must remain on the outside when you build your sandwiches and will create a lovely crunchy crust.
3 Fill your sandwiches with the chorizo, cheese slices, red onion and watercress, splitting the ingredients evenly between 4 sandwiches.
4 Place a dry frying pan on a medium heat. Add your sandwiches carefully to the pan and cook for 4 mins on each side. Use a spatula to press down and ensure the cheese melts but watch they don't burn.
5 Remove the sandwiches from the pan and serve with watercress on the side.

www.watercress.co.uk

6 SUNDAY

7 MONDAY

8 TUESDAY

9 WEDNESDAY

10 THURSDAY

11 FRIDAY

12 SATURDAY

A magical memory

WHEN LIFE WAS A HOLIDAY

Here I am with my daughters, Jane and Tina, on a beach in Saudi Arabia where my husband, David, had a job with British Aerospace. We lived at Al-Khobar on a compound for the British employees. There was a school which the children only attended in the mornings as it was too hot in the afternoons. Instead we went to the beach or to the pool where all the children learned to swim like fish. We had a Jeep to get around in and often went with friends to camp out on the beach overnight. We all wore flip-flops as it was impossible to walk on the sand with bare feet.

Every now and again a small plane would fly over the compound spraying insecticide and sometimes there were sandstorms when the whole house would be covered in a thin layer of sand. Lucky for us we had air-conditioning, as the heat would have been unbearable without it.

It was a wonderful carefree life, like a long holiday. Every six months the company paid for us to come home for a few weeks to be reunited with family and friends.
Josey Roofe, Gainsborough

Who am I?

Now best known for making cutting remarks to the rest of the Crawley family, I've previously worked magic in the Harry Potter movies, donned a nun's habit and won the 1969 Academy Award for my performance as a Scottish schoolteacher.

Maggie Smith

Nature diary

Become a beekeeper
With their skills as plant pollinators, keeping bees is a great hobby to start up come summer. Invest in proper beekeeping equipment and you can expect about 20-30lbs of honey a year from just one hive.

Make life easy

Make your own mini watering can using a plastic milk carton or large plastic bottle. Simply punch a few holes in the lid or the neck of your bottle, fill with water and you're set. Handy for indoor plants or doorstep pot plants when you don't feel like traipsing to get the watering can.

Quirky Britain

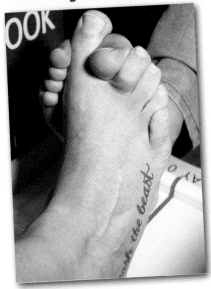

The World Toe Wrestling Championships, which is like arm wrestling but with feet, is held every summer in Ashbourne, Derbyshire. Opponents lock feet attempt to pin each other's foot down with no time limit. It consists of three rounds played with the right foot, then left and right again.

Recipe of the week

PILAFI WITH BROCCOLI, SOUR CHERRIES AND PISTACHIOS

SERVES: 4 PREP: 10 MINS COOK: 30 MINS

3 tbsp olive oil
3 cloves of garlic, sliced
2 onions, peeled and sliced
2 tbsp of tomato purée
200g (7oz) bulgur wheat
800ml (1½pt) vegetable stock
1 cinnamon stick
Sea salt and freshly ground black pepper
100g (3½oz) dried sour cherries
300g (10½oz) Tenderstem broccoli
1 lemon
½ bunch mint, leaves picked and roughly chopped
1 bunch flat-leaf parsley, leaves picked and roughly chopped
40g (1½oz) pistachios, chopped
Greek yogurt to serve

1 Place a large saucepan on a medium-low heat with the olive oil. Add the garlic and onions and sauté for 12-15 mins until softened.
2 Stir in the tomato purée followed by the bulgur wheat. Add the stock and cinnamon stick. Season generously and bring to the boil. Once boiling turn the heat to low and cover with a lid for 15 mins.
3 Halfway through cooking, stir the cherries into the pan and place the broccoli on top.
4 When the bulgur wheat is tender remove from the heat, cover with a tea towel and leave to one side for 20 mins. When the pilafi has cooled slightly, squeeze in the lemon juice and fluff up with a fork.
5 Stir through the herbs and serve with the pistachios scattered over the top and yogurt on the side.
www.tenderstem.co.uk

13 SUNDAY

14 MONDAY

15 TUESDAY

16 WEDNESDAY

17 THURSDAY

18 FRIDAY

19 SATURDAY

A magical memory

ANOTHER SUNNY HONEYMOON

When John and I were wed at a register office in Cornwall in June 1986, I told him that I would not feel really married unless we had a church blessing.

We went to Dorset for our honeymoon and I had a shock when I discovered that John had bought a watch that played The Wedding March all day and night on the hour! Our landlady was tickled pink and laughed: "So that's your little secret!" and picked a rosebud from her garden to complement my dress.

The Wedding March accompanied us through breakfast and on the boat over to Brownsea Island where John had once lived when he worked for Lady Bonham Christie. Unbeknown to me, he had previously contacted the Bishop of Crediton and arranged for us to have a blessing in the beautiful church of St Mary.

All was cool and silent in the church where we knelt before the altar and the vicar gave his blessing. It was an emotional 15 minutes. When we emerged into the brilliant sunlight, I smiled sweetly at John and said: "You can get rid of that watch, my darling. I'll call the tune now that we're wed!"

Diana Manning, Campbeltown

Who am I?

Born in Montreal, I was adopted at the age of four. But I soon found a passion for acting and made my name playing mother of a roast-dinner-loving family in a series of British adverts. Later I became a much-loved columnist for **Yours** magazine.

Lynda Bellingham

Nature diary

Beautiful biennials

Now is a great time to plant some bright and beautiful biennials in your garden. We love 'summer breeze orange' (Papaver nudicaule) that will open for many weeks during the summer months adding a vibrant orange colour to any garden.

Make life easy

Use a metal reusable straw to quickly and easily hull strawberries. Carefully insert the straw into the tip of the strawberry and push through to remove the stem in one easy and mess-free move. Great if you're chopping lots to make jam, or just as an easy-to-eat snack for children.

Quirky Britain

Swan Upping is a ceremony which occurs in the third week of July, in which mute swans on the River Thames are lifted out of the water, ringed, and then released - a tradition that dates back to the 12th Century. Its practical purpose today is to conduct a census of swans and check their health.

Recipe of the week

PUFF PASTRY BAKED EGG AND PESTO PARCELS

SERVES: 1 PREP: 10 MINS COOK: 20 MINS

Rolled puff pastry, roughly 15cm x 25cm rectangle
1 tbsp pesto
2 asparagus spears, trimmed and cut in half
30g (1oz) feta
2 medium British Lion eggs
2 slices prosciutto

1 Preheat the oven to 200°C/400°F/Gas Mark 6.
2 Cut the pastry in half into two square shapes. Make a frame out of one of the squares, cutting out a square in the middle and removing it gently. Place 'the frame' on top of the full square and press down gently.
2 Spread the pesto over the centre of the pastry (leaving the frame uncovered), place the asparagus on one side, prosciutto on the other and crumble the feta over the top, leaving a space in the middle for your egg. Brush the pastry frame with one egg yolk.
3 Put the pastry on a lined baking tray and bake for 10-15 mins, until puffed.
4 Remove from the oven and crack the whole egg into the centre. Put back in the oven for another 5 mins, until the egg white is set.
4 Serve with a side of green salad or sprinkling of seeds.
British Lion Eggs www.eggrecipes.co.uk

20 SUNDAY

21 MONDAY

22 TUESDAY

23 WEDNESDAY

24 THURSDAY

25 FRIDAY

26 SATURDAY

A magical memory

THE SUNDAY SCHOOL OUTING

At Sunday School, the pastor produced a large book in which the names of all the children and parents who were going on the annual outing were listed. I excitedly listened for 'the Fyson family' to be read out - we were on the second of the three coaches.

At last the day arrived and my mother prepared a packed lunch while my father packed everything we needed in a neat and tidy fashion. We arrived early to find several families already at the assembly point and were soon on our way to the coast. Several children started to tuck into their sweets and crisps. I could smell the egg sandwiches that were the favourite of a girl called Gillian. Everyone cheered when they saw the sea ahead.

After lunch, the fun began. In this photo, I am in the centre and my sister is the girl buried up to her neck in sand. The sea was cold but the sand was soft and warm.

An ice-cream was the final treat as the day came to an end and I tried to remove the sand from my shoes before I climbed back on to the coach for the journey home.
Christine Fyson, Ashford

Who am I?

I was the only actor to appear in all 295 episodes of a classic TV sitcom over 30 years. I also lent my well-loved voice to the Wallace and Gromit series and Rat in The Wind in the Willows.

Peter Sallis

Nature diary

Summer solstice

June 21 marks the Summer Solstice and there's no better time to embrace nature. Start your morning outdoors with a spot of yoga and meditation while the sun rises. Later in the day you could plan a barbecue with friends and family to celebrate summer.

Make life easy

Forget scrubbing your barbecue grill, instead let the heat do the hard work for you. Cut an onion in half and heat the barbecue until it's hot. Use a long-handled fork to rub the onion up and down over the grill until any grease and food debris lifts off.

Quirky Britain

On the **Summer Solstice at Stonehenge** thousands of people gather around the monument to watch the sunrise (approximately 4.52am) in celebration of the first day of summer - a tradition believed to have been practised at the site thousands of years ago by the Neolithic people.

Recipe of the week

BAKED PEPPERS WITH RICE, CHICKEN AND WALNUTS

SERVES: 4 PREP: 20 MINS COOK: 30 MINS

1 tbsp olive oil
150g (5oz) chestnut mushrooms, sliced
250g (9oz) pouch microwave sun-dried tomato basmati rice
50g (2oz) California Walnut Pieces, roughly chopped
200g (7oz) cooked roast chicken, shredded
½ x 25g (10z) pack parsley, chopped
4 red peppers

1 Preheat the oven to 200°C/400°F/Gas Mark 6.
2 Heat the oil in a frying pan and fry the mushrooms for 3-4 mins. Add the rice, walnuts and chicken and fry for 2-3 mins until heated through. Season to taste and stir in the parsley and 2-3 tbsp water.
3 Cut the tops off the peppers and remove the seeds. Trim the bases if needed so they stand upright and place them in a small roasting tin with 3 tbsp water in the base.
4 Spoon the rice mixture into the pepper shells and bake for 30 mins or until the peppers are just softened.
5 Serve with a fresh leafy salad.
www.californiawalnuts.co.uk

27 SUNDAY

28 MONDAY

29 TUESDAY

30 WEDNESDAY

1 THURSDAY

2 FRIDAY

3 SATURDAY

A magical memory

LOVING LIFE IN NORFOLK

When I was young money was tight, but my dad saved small change in a sweet jar and once a year it was emptied out so that we could have a holiday at the seaside. How I loved that week away! No school, no rules, just heavenly days on the beach, shell-seeking and swimming. We had picnics every day and there was a 'yes!' to ice-cream or candy floss for afters. This picture of me was taken around 1965 and it was the photo that cheered me up on the dark winter days when I longed for summer again and the next holiday in Norfolk.

When I grew up and met my husband, I discovered that his family had holidayed in Norfolk too, but on the Broads, not the coast. So I tried life on a boat and he tried life in a chalet, and we loved them both. We promised each other we would move to Norfolk one day.

We introduced our children to the joys of seaside holidays and even though our daughter went off to live in New Zealand, she returned here to have a Norfolk wedding. Now her husband loves it, too.

Ginette Pooley, Norfolk

Who am I?

When I started my career in the Eighties, I hoped I wasn't just another 'pretty' face. Often voted the world's most beautiful woman, I was Hugh Grant's crush in a 1999 film and won an Oscar for my role as Erin Brockovich.

Julia Roberts

Nature diary

Time for compost

The summer months are great for hot composting your weeds as the hotter the temperature, the quicker the weeds can compost. Ensure your compost bin is in a very sunny location and turn the heap on a regular basis.

Make life easy

Wash your home grown veg in the garden and avoid bringing the mud into the house with this clever tip. Simply drill some holes in the bottom and sides of a bucket to create a giant colander, then use a hose to clean them off.

Quirky Britain

The small English village of Willaston hosts a yearly competition (typically on a Saturday in late June) known as the **World Worm Charming Championships**, where competitors come from far and wide to try to convince as many worms as they can to rise to the surface, which are then released back to nature after dark.

Recipe of the week

STRAWBERRY BISCOFF CHEESECAKE

SERVES: 6 PREP: 90 MINS FRIDGE: OVERNIGHT

200g (7oz) Lotus Biscoff Biscuits
100g (3½oz) butter
1 egg
1.5kg (3.3lb) hulled strawberries
500g (1lb 2oz) soft cheese
3 limes, zested and juiced
250ml (½pt) whipping cream
3 gelatine leaves, soaked in cold water and squeezed dry.

1 Preheat the oven to 180°C/ 350°F/ Gas Mark 4.
2 Crumble the Biscoff and mix with the butter and egg. Press the mixture firmly into a 19cm loose-bottomed tin.
3 Bake in the oven for 15 mins, then leave to cool.
4 Cut the strawberries in half and place them in the baking tin with the top facing down and the cut side facing out. Keep some aside for garnishing.
5 Mix the soft cheese and lime zest in a large bowl. Whip the cream and add to the soft cheese.
6 Put the lime juice in a small saucepan and heat gently. Dissolve the gelatine in the juice.
7 Pour the lime and gelatine mix into the soft cheese and mix gently. Spoon this mixture into the baking tin.
8 Garnish with the remaining strawberries and refrigerate for 24 hours to become firm.
www.lotusbiscoff.com

4 SUNDAY

5 MONDAY

6 TUESDAY

7 WEDNESDAY

8 THURSDAY

9 FRIDAY

10 SATURDAY

A magical memory

OUR VERY OWN BEACH HUT

Here is the Huggins family pictured on one of our many happy holidays spent at Sandown on the Isle of Wight. I am kneeling between my mum and Auntie Agg. My sister has the bucket and spade. I can't help smiling now at the ribbons in our hair and the white sandals.

It took nearly a whole day to get to Sandown from Tottenham. We took a train to Liverpool Street and another to Southampton, then the ferry over to the island and a little steam train to Sandown where we stayed with Mr and Mrs Eiger at Royal Crescent.

We always hired a beach hut where we could make tea and sandwiches. I remember the sand being so hot it burned our feet. Our swimsuits were knitted – disastrous when wet!

Two of my favourite places were Blackgang Chine and Shanklin Chine. We used to walk to Sandown Golf Club, crossing over little stiles. On the way we passed some brick walls into which we inserted halfpennies where the cement was missing. I often wonder if they are still there. Happy memories!

Valerie Temple, Great Dunmow

Who am I?

Mother to Princess Leia, I'm a belle of Hollywood's golden age, having tap danced with Gene Kelly. In 1969 I had my own TV show, later founded my own dance studios and was an avid collector of film memorabilia.

Debbie Reynolds

Nature diary

Look after your lawn

Now is a great time to give your lawn a boost with some grass fertiliser to make it even more lush and green. If the weather has been dry, be sure to set your mower blades higher to reduce stress on the grass.

Make life easy

Ants coming into your home? Instead of ant powder use cinnamon powder, a natural alternative, which you can sprinkle along any entry points. Ants hate the smell! Cinnamon essential oil works well too, when applied to the same high traffic areas. Keep all essential oils away from pets, however.

Quirky Britain

Hosted by the Bottle Inn pub in Dorset each July, the **World Nettle Eating Championships** sees dozens of competitors take part in eating as many nettle stalks as possible within one hour. The winners typically eat around 70ft of nettle stalks which are said to cause a tingling feeling in the mouth.

Recipe of the week

JAPANESE SAVOURY PANCAKE WITH TENDERSTEM BROCCOLI

SERVES: 2 PREP: 20 MINS COOK: 20 MINS

300g (10½oz) Tenderstem broccoli, roughly chopped
150g (5oz) plain flour
1¼ tsp salt
4 medium eggs
200g (7oz) red cabbage, thinly shredded
6 spring onions, sliced on an angle
2 tbsp rapeseed oil
To serve:
2 tbsp mayonnaise
Okonomiyaki sauce (or mix 2 tbsp Worcestershire sauce, 1 tbsp ketchup, 1 tsp soy sauce, 1 tsp honey)
Japanese beni-shoga (pickled ginger)

1 Blanch the broccoli by boiling it for 3 mins. Drain and set aside to cool.
2 With a fork, whisk the flour, salt, eggs and 150ml (¼pt) water together in a mixing bowl until your batter is lump free.
3 Add the red cabbage, the white part of the spring onions and the broccoli to the batter. Mix well.
4 Prepare the toppings. Mix the mayonnaise with a little water, so that you can drizzle it with a spoon. Set the sauce and pickled ginger aside.
5 Heat 1 tbsp of oil in a small frying pan over a medium to high heat. Add half the batter to the pan and flatten it with a spoon or spatula, it should be around 3cm deep. Cook for 4 mins until you can see the scraps of cabbage and batter starting to brown and crisp. After 4 mins, turn and cook on the other side for a further 3 mins. When cooked through turn out onto a plate. Repeat with the remaining batter.
6 To serve, drizzle over the okonomiyaki sauce, then the mayonnaise, before topping with the pickled ginger and remaining spring onion greens.
www.tenderstem.co.uk

11 SUNDAY

12 MONDAY

13 TUESDAY

14 WEDNESDAY

15 THURSDAY

16 FRIDAY

17 SATURDAY

A magical memory

GARDENING IN THE GENES

This photo of my mum and dad in their lovingly tended front garden is a precious fragment of my past that seems like only yesterday. Dad always enjoyed filling both the front and back garden with the flowers which were his passion. Even before he retired, when he was working full time, he would be out there as much as possible, planting vegetables as well as flowers. He used to enter his chrysanthemums in the local horticultural shows. While he was busy in the garden, Mum would be indoors, baking. They weren't well off, but I could always feel their love for each other. They were married in 1942 and had 66 years together, both living into their 90s.

I miss them dearly but am very happy that Dad's passion has rubbed off on me and my granddaughter. She has an allotment near where she lives in Newcastle while I have my own small garden. I also help by volunteering at Horatio's Garden near to the spinal unit of Stoke Mandeville hospital.
Pauline Patterson, Aylesbury

Who am I?

Born in Los Angeles, 1937, I wanted to go into medicine but quit college to pursue acting. Maybe I didn't 'graduate' but once I started making movies in 1967, I received other accolades including six Best Actor Oscar nominations.

Dustin Hoffman

Nature diary

Hooray for butterflies

Watch the garden light up with colour courtesy of some special summer guests. Gatekeepers, large whites and meadow browns are some of the most popular garden butterflies but you can attract more by growing foods such as marigolds, garden mint, lavender and marjoram.

Make life easy

Struggling to sleep in the summer heat? A dead easy trick is to pop your pillowcases in the freezer an hour or so before bedtime. Then simply put them back on your pillows and you'll find them instantly cooling and refreshing before hitting the hay.

Quirky Britain

Ready, steady, slow! Around 200 snails compete in the **World Snail Racing Championships** - part of the Congham Fete, in Norfolk. The region has hosted snail racing for more than 25 years. Entrants race over a 13 inch course in the fastest time possible, over the watchful eye of a snail trainer.

Recipe of the week

CHOCOLATE, ORANGE AND WATERCRESS BROWNIES WITH CHOCOLATE GANACHE

MAKES: 16 SQUARES PREP: 40 MINS COOK: 40 MINS

300g (10½oz) dark chocolate, chopped
200g (7oz) unsalted butter
Zest of one orange
350g (12oz) caster sugar
4 large eggs
100g (3½oz) plain flour, sieved
50g (2oz) cocoa powder, sieved
50g (2oz) watercress, finely chopped
For the ganache:
250g (9oz) good quality dark chocolate, chopped
250ml (½pt) double cream
1 tbsp Cointreau (optional)

1 Preheat the oven to 180°C/ 350°F/ Gas Mark 4. Line a square brownie tin with greaseproof paper.
2 Place 200g (7oz) of the chocolate, the butter and the orange zest in a heatproof bowl and melt in the microwave for 30 seconds, stirring and repeating until melted.
3 Use an electric whisk to beat together the eggs and sugar until pale and fluffy. Leave the chocolate mixture to cool for five mins before stirring into the egg mix, then mix in the flour and cocoa.
4 Stir in the remaining chocolate and the watercress, then pour into the prepared tin. Bake for 35-40 mins. Remove from the oven and leave to cool.
5 Make the ganache topping. Gently bring the double cream to the boil in a saucepan. Remove from the heat, stir in the chocolate until melted and mixed thoroughly. Stir in the Cointreau if using.
6 Allow the ganache to cool slightly, then pour over the brownies while still in the tin. Smooth the topping out and leave for 30 mins before cutting into squares.
www.watercress.co.uk

18 SUNDAY

19 MONDAY

20 TUESDAY

21 WEDNESDAY

22 THURSDAY

23 FRIDAY

24 SATURDAY

A magical memory

APPLE BLOSSOM ALLERGY

The couple in the photo are Harry and Renie Burns who were the parents of my friend, Jan. Harry had promised us that when the M1, England's first motorway opened, he would take us on a trip and he did just that in the summer of 1959 when we had left school.

As we were fans of the poet and hymn writer William Cowper, we travelled to visit his home in Olney, Buckinghamshire. After visiting the house, we found a place to have a picnic. Jan and I freshened up with our favourite perfume, Apple Blossom by Helena Rubinstein. Unfortunately, this caused her father to have a coughing fit as soon as we got back in the car. He insisted that we should get out again so we all waited for half an hour with all the windows wide open before we could drive home.

After this incident, he refused to take us out anywhere again until he had checked what perfume we were using before we set off. He was a lovely man and Jan and I remained close friends in contact every day until she sadly passed away eleven years ago.
Margaret O'Callaghan, Wolverhampton

Who am I?

Working in printing aged 15, I found my way into a singing audition, adopted the Mod look and released An Old Raincoat Won't Ever Let You Down. I'm now married to a leggy model and have a model railway hobby.

Sir Rod Stewart

Nature diary

Feed flying friends

With all this hot weather, it's important to keep the birds that visit our garden well fed and watered. Offer them a range of foods including berries, seeds and nuts and keep the bird bath topped up well with water.

Make life easy

Chill a bottle of wine quicker by wrapping it in damp kitchen roll and placing it in the freezer. Why not also freeze grapes and add them to your glass to chill your spritzer, as a tasty and easy alternative to ice-cubes?

Quirky Britain

Step onto the gangplank and leave the real world behind as you descend below the water line (wellies not necessary) and enter a magical 50-seat theatre on a converted barge, which presents marionette and puppet spectacles throughout the year from moorings at **Little Venice and Richmond**, London, during the summer.

Recipe of the week

VEGGIE SLIDER BURGERS WITH HORSERADISH MAYO

SERVES: 4 PREP: 15 MINS COOK: 25 MINS

400g (14oz) tin cannellini beans, drained
2 tbsp olive oil
1 small red onion, diced
2 garlic cloves, crushed
1 x 180g pack Love Beets Cooked Beetroot, chopped into 1cm cubes
125g (4½oz) cooked mixed grains such as bulgur wheat and quinoa
30g (1oz) breadcrumbs
15g (½oz) dill, chopped
15g (½oz) flat-leaf parsley, chopped
6 tbsp mayonnaise
3 tbsp creamed horseradish sauce
4 Brioche burger buns, cut sides lightly toasted or griddled
40g (1½oz) watercress, to serve
2 gherkins, sliced, to serve (optional)

1 Add the beans to a bowl and mash to a paste with some texture remaining.
2 Add 1 tbsp oil to a frying pan, set over a low-medium heat then add the onion and cook for 10 mins, stirring occasionally until soft and translucent. Stir in the garlic and cook for 2 mins more. Stir in the beetroot and set aside to cool.
3 Add the cooled beetroot and onion mix to the mashed beans with the mixed grains, breadcrumbs and herbs. Season generously.
4 Shape the mix into 4 equal-sized patties and chill until ready to cook.
5 Add the mayonnaise and horseradish to a bowl, stir and season to taste.
6 Brush the patties with the remaining oil and griddle on the barbecue (or fry in a pan) until golden and charred on both sides.
7 Serve the burgers in buns with horseradish mayonnaise, watercress and gherkins.
www.lovebeets.co.uk

25 SUNDAY

26 MONDAY

27 TUESDAY

28 WEDNESDAY

29 THURSDAY

30 FRIDAY

31 SATURDAY

A magical memory

NORTH OF THE BORDER

One of my most treasured memories is of my first visit to Scotland in the summer of 1989. This picture of me sitting down to enjoy the view was taken in the botanical gardens in Dumfries on the West coast. I was six months pregnant at the time and I am wearing a maternity dress made by my lovely mum, Dorothy. As it was a very hot summer my husband, John, had driven us from our home in the Midlands to the North where it was cooler.

Thanks to the Gulf stream and its sheltered location, many plants from warmer climes flourished in the garden. While we were there, we spent some of our time trying to decide on a name for our first child. After much deliberation, and inspired by the small shrub that commonly grows in Scotland, we agreed that if we had a girl we would call her Heather. And three months later, on October 31, she came into the world.

Scotland remains a very special place. We have been back several times and recently enjoyed a lovely cruise around its islands.
Chris Wileman, Walsall

Who am I?

Starting my career on New Faces, I became good friends of Julie Walters and Celia Imrie. We had a lot of fun together dabbling in antiques and serving in a canteen. I later wrote the serious drama Housewife, 49.

Victoria Wood

Nature diary

Keep herbs happy

Herb gardens are a great addition to any garden, especially if you love to cook. But they need treating carefully. Allow herbs at least 4 hours of sunlight a day and water only when the soil feels dry to the touch.

Make life easy

Cook fish al fresco with this tasty tip. Add a layer of sliced lemons between the fish and the barbecue. Not only will they help prevent the fish sticking or falling down the gaps, lemon adds a delicious flavour to any meats and vegetables you're cooking.

Quirky Britain

At 46 metres tall, **The Old Lighthouse** in Dungeness, Kent, is a great place for enjoying panoramic views over the English Channel and surrounding countryside. But with 169 steps to the top, it's certainly not for the faint-hearted! Inside, you'll find out how a lighthouse works and read the stories of the people who used to operate it.

Recipe of the week

SPICY BRITISH TOMATO, CHICKPEA AND AVOCADO SALAD

SERVES: 4 PREP: 10 MINS COOK: 10 MINS

100g (3½oz) bulgur wheat
2 tsp vegetable stock powder (or half a vegetable stock cube)
400g (14oz) can chickpeas, rinsed and drained
200g (7oz) British cherry or baby plum tomatoes, halved
2 ripe avocados, peeled, pitted and sliced
1 yellow pepper, deseeded and sliced
80g (3oz) bag spinach, rocket and watercress salad
1 tsp cumin seeds
2 tbsp mixed seeds
3 tbsp olive oil
2 tbsp lemon juice
1tsp Dijon mustard
Pinch of salt, pepper and sugar

1 Cook the bulgur wheat according to pack instructions, flavouring the cooking water with the vegetable stock.
2 Mix together the chickpeas, tomatoes, avocados and pepper. Rinse the cooked bulgur wheat with cold water and drain. Add to the tomato mixture and season.
3 Share the salad leaves between 4 serving plates and top with the tomato mixture. Toast the cumin seeds and mixed seeds in a dry frying pan until lightly browned. Sprinkle over the salads.
4 Make the dressing. Mix together the olive oil, lemon juice and mustard. Season with a pinch of salt, pepper and sugar. Sprinkle over the salads and serve.

British Tomato Grower's Association www.britishtomatoes.co.uk

1 SUNDAY

2 MONDAY

3 TUESDAY

4 WEDNESDAY

5 THURSDAY

6 FRIDAY

7 SATURDAY

A magical memory

DISCOVERING MY PAST

One warm July day as I travelled through the Lake District on the way to my mother's house, I noticed the large, red lamppost poppies. Each one commemorated a soldier who fell in the First World War. I was struck by how many there were and how often there were several poppies for members of the same family.

As I drove into the village where my mother had been born and where she lived for most of her life, the names on the poppies were very familiar. One of the three hanging by the school gates bore the words, 'Remembering James Smith'. He was my great-grandfather (pictured above). I felt very proud, but also ashamed that I knew so little about him.

I felt inspired to learn more about the character I had only known through fireside chats when I was a child. I found photographs of him and details of his life through family documents. During my search, I came across a studio photo of a smart young lady who was James's sister. Written on the back were the words, 'Lost at sea. Either the Titanic or the Lusitania'.

Angela Borrowdale, Windermere

Who am I?

I shared a stage with Judy Garland, Debbie Reynolds and Jerry the mouse over the years. My last movie was Xanadu starring Olivia Newton-John, but you'll know me best for splashing round the drainpipes on a particularly soggy evening.

Gene Kelly

Nature diary

Light up the garden

As we're spending more of our evenings outside, spruce up your garden with a touch of lighting. Solar lights that stick in the soil don't add to the electricity while hanging fairy lights add a magical touch around your garden.

Make life easy

Freeze leftover herbs or avoid food waste by chopping them finely and either freezing them in bags, or in ice cube trays with a little water. The herb cubes are perfect for adding to soups and stews and frozen mint cubes are delicious added to Pimm's and cocktails!

Quirky Britain

On the first Saturday each August, the Derbyshire town of Bonsall hosts the **World Hen Racing Championship**. This quirky race sees hens competing over a 20-yard course, with just four minutes to make their way to the finish line in a series of timed heats - a tradition dating back more than 100 years.

Recipe of the week

APPLE PIE BREAKFAST SMOOTHIE BOWL

SERVES: 3 PREP: 10 MINS

For the smoothie:
1 frozen banana, peeled
250g (9oz) of unsweetened soya yogurt
1 Pink Lady apple, cored and cut into chunks
75g (3oz) oats
2 tbsp chia or flax seeds
2 tsp ground cinnamon
2 tsp vanilla extract
200ml (7fl oz) fortified, unsweetened soya or almond milk
2 tsp of freeze-dried raspberry powder (optional)
For the topping:
1 Pink Lady apple, cored and
sliced
1 tbsp chia or flax seeds
3 tbsp pomegranate seeds
Edible flowers (optional)

1 Place all the smoothie ingredients in a high-speed blender until smooth and creamy. Pour into bowls.
2 Top with the apple slices, chia or flax seeds, pomegranate seeds or flowers (if using) and serve immediately.
www.pinkladyapples.co.uk

8 SUNDAY

9 MONDAY

10 TUESDAY

11 WEDNESDAY

12 THURSDAY

13 FRIDAY

14 SATURDAY

A magical memory

FIRST DAY AT SCHOOL

The year was 1949, I was five years' old and starting my first term at the Blessed Sacrament Convent School. As my father had been killed on active service during the war, the RAF helped to pay the school fees.

I looked very smart in my black gymslip, white blouse, striped tie, long grey socks and black shoes. My hair was long and my mother used to style it in ringlets, wrapping it in strips of rag every night before I went to bed.

On my first day, the nuns greeted us children at the door and ushered us into the hall, then into the cloakroom to hang up our coats before showing us to our classrooms. All seemed to go well, until lunchtime when I decided to walk home. Luckily, it was in the same road as the school so I made it safely to the front door and sat down on the steps.

My mother happened to open the door and found me there. She must have been horrified! I was given some lunch then quickly marched back to school. It was the only time it happened, but I remember it well.

Jacqueline Pomeroy, Brighton

Who am I?

Originally from the US, I became a Swiss citizen in 2013. I'm known for my powerful voice and energetic stage presence which meant I was often referred to as the Queen of Rock 'n' Roll. Some would say I'm the best.

Tina Turner

Nature diary

Do your bit for moths

Although they rarely get as much love as butterflies, moths are a very important part of the food chain, not to mention their incredible markings and colours. Help them by planting some moth-friendly nectar-rich plants such as jasmine or honeysuckle.

Make life easy

When packing for summer holidays, here's a handy tip to stop shoes catching on your clothes or making them dirty. Simply save and use the complimentary shower caps from hotel bathrooms to cover the bottoms of shoes in your suitcase and the rest of your items will stay lovely and clean.

Quirky Britain

Situated in the heart of Lincolnshire, **Heckington Windmill** is the only working eight-sailed windmill of its type in the world, producing stone ground flour. Explore all of its five floors on a guided tour to learn about milling and the stories that lie behind its 189-year history.

Recipe of the week

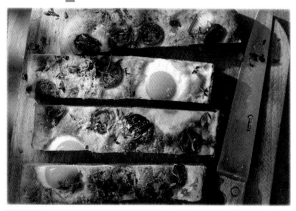

BREAKFAST FOCACCIA WITH BAKED EGGS

SERVES: 10 PREP: 45 MINS COOK: 10 MINS

400g (14oz) bread flour
1 sachet of activated dried yeast
1 tsp salt
1 tsp caster sugar
250ml (9fl oz) lukewarm water
3-5 large British Lion eggs
150g (5oz) cherry tomatoes, halved
60g (2½oz) pitted olives, halved
5 springs of thyme
30g (1oz) parmesan, grated
Salt
Olive oil

1 Preheat the oven to 200°C/400°F/Gas Mark 6.
2 Mix together the flour, yeast, salt and sugar. Make a well in the middle and pour in half of the water. Knead until the ingredients are combined. Add the rest of the water and knead for 5 mins until the dough is smooth and springy.
3 Cover with a damp cloth and leave in a warm place for 30 mins, until the dough doubles in size.
4 Transfer onto a deep roasting tray (32cm x 20cm or smaller). Stretch to the sides and push down with your fingers making small dwells.
5 Drizzle generously with olive oil. Make 3-5 egg size balls with tin foil and press them onto the dough.
6 Use tomatoes, olives and thyme to fill the gaps between the foil balls. Press all the toppings down into the dough. Sprinkle the parmesan over and leave for 20 mins.
7 Bake for 15 mins, until golden brown. Remove the foil balls and crack an egg into each hole. Bake for 5 mins or until the egg whites are set.
8 Serve with a drizzle of olive oil and a sprinkling of salt.

British Lion Eggs www.eggrecipes.co.uk

15 SUNDAY

16 MONDAY

17 TUESDAY

18 WEDNESDAY

19 THURSDAY

20 FRIDAY

21 SATURDAY

A magical memory

NICK AND THE STOLEN PEACHES

When I was six, my ten-year-old brother Nick was my hero so I wanted to prove worthy of being his second-in-command. The goal was our neighbour's hothouse full of a crop of delicious peaches. We squeezed into the roof gully between our sheds and the hothouse. Nick carefully lowered our father's fishing basket and handed the end of the line to me: "Hold it steady, Mary. Don't let go." Using a stick, he began to knock peaches into the basket, but my already strained arms couldn't hold the load and down it went.

We were subdued over supper and I didn't sleep well that night. Nick put on a brave show and said he didn't care. When we came down for breakfast, there was a surprise waiting for us on the kitchen table. There was our basket filled with fruit. Pinned to it was a note, 'I would have happily given you these if you had only asked'.

My mother took us next door to apologise. Then she made us eat a peach with every meal until they were finished. To this day, just looking at a peach makes me feel sick!
Mary Holford-Walker, via email

Who am I?

My surname changed from Cheese when my father joined the army. Now I'm best known for the Seventies sitcom I co-wrote with my wife. One of the Monty Python boys, I've guest-starred in the Muppet Show and a Bond movie.

John Cleese

Nature diary

Prune wisteria

Now is a good time to do your summer pruning of wisteria. Start by cutting down the long shoots to just 6 inches each and tidy up the rest. Avoid bumping the flowerbuds as they're very fragile and may fall off.

Make life easy

Create your own garden markers using stones or pebbles and paint. Perfect for involving the grandchildren, use acrylic paints to make your design and once dry, seal with a waterproof outdoor varnish then pop in pride of place. Be as creative as you like!

Quirky Britain

The Lost Gardens of Heligan are one of the most mysterious green spaces in England. At 200 acres in size, it features a valley of sub-tropical plants, a vegetable garden and a Giant's Head (shown) and the Mud Maid - a sleeping woman of the forest made out of wood, grass, and earth.

Recipe of the week

ICE-CREAM CAKE WITH BISCOFF, MERINGUE AND CHOCOLATE

SERVES: 6 PREP: 30 MINS FREEZE: 4 HOURS

60g (2½oz) mixed nuts, eg hazelnuts and almonds
60g (2½oz) Lotus Biscoff biscuits
20g (¾oz) butter
4 tbsp sugar
1 tsp ground cinnamon
4 tbsp vegetable oil
600g (1lb 5oz) whipping cream
8g (2 tsp) vanilla sugar
100g (3½oz) ready-made meringues
200g (7oz) milk chocolate

1 Preheat the oven to 180°C/350°F/Gas Mark 4.
2 Toast the nuts lightly and chop them finely. Crumble the Biscoff. Melt the butter. Mix the nuts, Biscoff, sugar and cinnamon together. Add the oil and melted butter and mix well.
3 Put this mixture into a loose-bottomed baking tin and press firmly. Bake the base in the oven for 10 mins and leave to cool.
4 Whip the cream with the vanilla sugar and icing sugar. Crumble the meringues and fold into the cream using a spatula.
5 Put the cream into the baking tin and place in the freezer for at least 4 hours.
6 Melt the milk chocolate in a bain-marie and pour over the ice-cream cake just before serving.
www.lotusbiscoff.com

22 SUNDAY

23 MONDAY

24 TUESDAY

25 WEDNESDAY

26 THURSDAY

27 FRIDAY

28 SATURDAY

A magical memory

HAPPY TIMES AT HOME

Our family home was a three-bedroom semi-detached house with a very large garden. Sadly, after 55 years it had to be sold when my father's health declined and he had to move into a care home. My mother now lives in a warden-controlled flat nearby. We spent many happy, carefree summers in that house, playing bowls on the lawn and table tennis in the garage. When we were children there used to be a coal bunker in the garden and I remember getting my dressing-up clothes very dirty in there! Later, my four-year-old grandson loved splashing around in the paddling pool.

Our parents grew fruit and vegetables as well as flowers, especially roses. We held many 'open garden' events to raise funds for Mum's church. Members of the congregation came to admire the plants and enjoy tea and cake. Over the years, especially at Christmas, we had many large family parties when Mum would produce a magnificent buffet. We will always miss our special home but no-one can take away these memories.
Hilary Biggs, via email

Who am I?

I was in a popular soap opera in my native country but went on to be the Princess of Pop, selling 70 million records worldwide. I was lucky to also star in several films including Moulin Rouge and Street Fighter.

Kylie Minogue

Nature diary
Listen to crickets
The sound of crickets in the countryside is one of the highlights of summer. As evening falls, head to a comfy spot in your garden and listen out. The sound is created when the male cricket rubs his back legs together to entice a female.

Make life easy
Always ending up with mismatched or odd earrings in your jewellery box? Place your earrings through the holes of a button to keep pairs safely together. Medication pill boxes are also really handy for securely storing your earrings when travelling.

Quirky Britain

Set at the foot of the **Cuillin Mountains** on the Isle of Skye, these mystical rock pools look like something out of a Scottish fairytale. On a sunny day, the waters are so clear that you can see each moss-covered stone at the bottom. In wetter weather, torrents of water whirl in thunderous cascades.

Recipe of the week

APPLE AND MOROCCAN GIANT COUSCOUS SALAD

SERVES: 2 PREP: 10 MINS COOK: 10 MINS

3 tbsp dry sherry
50g (2oz) sultanas or raisins
200g (7oz) giant couscous
1 tsp smoked paprika
¼ tsp ground cinnamon
½ tsp ground cumin
1 Pink Lady apple, cored and diced
2 shallots, finely chopped
1 garlic clove, crushed
2 tsp fresh root ginger, finely grated
½ red chilli, de-seeded and finely chopped
25g (1oz) fresh mint leaves, finely chopped
Grated zest of 1 lemon
1 tbsp pine nuts, toasted

1 Put the sherry into a small saucepan and gently bring just below the boil. Add the sultanas and set aside to soak.
2 Meanwhile put the couscous into a saucepan of boiling water and simmer for 6-8 mins until swollen and tender. Drain in a sieve and rinse in cold water. Drain again and use the base of a bowl to squeeze out any excess liquid. Set aside.
3 Put the paprika, cinnamon and cumin into a dry frying pan and gently heat until fragrant. Transfer to a large bowl. Add all the remaining ingredients and stir in the couscous, sultanas and soaking sherry. Check seasoning and serve.

www.pinkladyapples.co.uk

29 SUNDAY

30 MONDAY

31 TUESDAY

1 WEDNESDAY

2 THURSDAY

3 FRIDAY

4 SATURDAY

A magical memory

SEDGEFIELD SARAH MAKES NEWS

I felt mixed emotions of pride and relief as I crossed the finishing line after participating in the BUPA Great North Run in September 2010. As a 'fun' runner, my choice of costume was inspired by the memory of my late Uncle Albert, my father's brother. For many

PICTURE REPRODUCED WITH PERMISSION FROM THE NORTHERN ECHO

years Albert had produced and starred in the Wrexham pantomime with all profits going to the orthopaedic ward of the local hospital. He was awarded the British Empire Medal for his charitable work and the ward is still called the Pantomime ward.

This is why I decided to run dressed as a pantomime dame who was called Sedgefield Sarah. Traditionally, Sarah is a cook so my outfit featured cupcakes and fairy cakes.

With 38,250 runners lined up to start the race, the atmosphere was fantastic. The Red Arrows flew overhead and local heroes, Ant and Dec, acted as starters. Enthusiastic crowds lined the 13-mile route and their gifts of refreshments were very welcome to stragglers like me.

My joy in raising money for The Alzheimer's Society was even greater when The Northern Echo featured this photo of me on the following day.

John Nicholls, Sedgefield

Who am I?

Named Terrence at birth, I was better known by my middle name. Considered the King of Cool, I loved motorcycles and in the late Fifties starred in the TV western Wanted: Dead or Alive and the 1970 film Bullitt.

Steve McQueen

Nature diary

Help the bees
If the weather has been on the warmer side, offer bees a safe haven to quench their thirst by putting out shallow dishes of water around the garden filled with pebbles so it's not too deep for them to get a drink.

Make life easy

Protect your powder make-up when travelling by placing a flat cotton wool pad in between the make-up and lid. Check the lid closes properly, then wrap in cling film so it's all nicely secure. That way you'll have no nasty breakages when you unpack your suitcase on arrival.

Quirky Britain

The World Bog Snorkelling Championship in Llanwrtyd Wells, Wales, takes place on August Bank Holiday and involves completing two consecutive laps of a trench filled with water cut through a peat bog. The competitor who completes the two lengths in the shortest time is the winner – but no conventional swimming strokes are allowed.

Recipe of the week

VEGAN CHOCOLATE MOUSSE

SERVES: 4 PREP: 5 MINS CHILL TIME: 2 HOURS

300g (10½oz) soft (Silken) tofu
60g (2½oz) dark chocolate (70 per cent minimum)
1 tbsp cocoa powder
2 tbsp maple syrup
1 tsp vanilla bean paste
Pinch of salt
GARNISH:
Raspberries
Hazelnuts
Cocoa nibs

1 Melt the dark chocolate over a bain-marie or in the microwave for 1-2 mins until just melted.
2 Place all the ingredients in a food processor and blitz until smooth.
3 Taste and adjust sweetness to taste.
4 Spoon into small ramekins and place in the fridge for 2 hours to set.
5 Remove from the fridge and garnish with fruits, nuts, granola of your choice.

Annabel Wray and Victoria Knight, professional chefs and co-founders of Hakuna Foods

5 SUNDAY

6 MONDAY

7 TUESDAY

8 WEDNESDAY

9 THURSDAY

10 FRIDAY

11 SATURDAY

A magical memory

FRIENDS FROM SCHOOLDAYS

This photo was taken when my friends and I were about to take our school certificate examination in 1949. I am second from the left. We six girls met when we first started school together and have remained close friends ever since then.

Although we sadly lost one of our number, Margaret, to dementia a few years ago, the remaining five of us continue to meet as often as we possibly can.

We chat to each other on the phone regularly, exchanging news of our families and what we've been up to. We all have children and grandchildren and some of us even have great-grandchildren. Elsie has family in Australia, June in New Zealand and Pat in Canada, so we have lots of news to exchange when we meet up. Although Elsie and I still live in Gravesend, the others are scattered across the country but we try to meet up on our birthdays each year.

We have also managed to enjoy some lovely weekends away at the seaside over the years, including one particularly memorable one in Whitstable.
Jean Gibbs, Gravesend

Who am I?

I'm a Texan actress who first came to fame in the film The Whole Wide World but I later achieved critical acclaim playing a hopelessly unlucky in love character in films based on the works of author Helen Fielding.

Renée Zellweger

Nature diary

Clean out bird nests

Now the nesting season is over, clean out nest boxes to prepare for the next visitors. Use boiling water to kill off any nasty germs and let the box dry out before replacing the lid. Legally you can only remove unhatched eggs from September to January.

Make life easy

If your hands are a little shaky, or you're not too confident when hammering in nails or picture hooks, save your fingers with this clever DIY trick. Use a peg or a pair of thin nosed pliers to help hold the nail still while you bang it in with the hammer.

Quirky Britain

Grab your dancing shoes! Set in Staffordshire, the **Abbots Bromley horn dance** is believed to be the oldest folk dance in Britain, dating back to the Middle Ages. It's performed annually on Wake Monday in September and features characters including deer-men, a fool, a hobby horse, a bowman and Maid Marian.

Recipe of the week

BOILED EGG CHICKEN SALAD

SERVES: 4 PREP: 15 MINS COOK: 30 MINS

2 tbsp soy sauce
1 tbsp maple syrup
1 tbsp rice wine vinegar
2 garlic cloves, peeled and finely chopped
5cm ginger, peeled and finely chopped
6 skinless chicken thighs
300g (10½oz) new potatoes, halved
1 tsp sesame oil
300ml (10fl oz) chicken stock
4 medium British Lion eggs
50g (2oz) salad leaves
50g (2oz) sugar snap peas, trimmed and sliced
1 carrot, peeled and julienned

1 To make the marinade, combine the soy sauce, maple syrup, rice wine vinegar, chopped garlic and ginger. Add the chicken thighs and set aside.
2 Cook the potatoes until soft.
3 Heat the sesame oil in a deep heavy-based frying pan over a medium heat. Add the chicken (save the marinade) and brown the meat on both sides. Add the chicken stock and the marinade. Cover with a lid, lower the heat and simmer for 15 mins.
4 While the chicken is cooking, bring a saucepan of water to a boil and carefully drop in the eggs. Boil for 5-6 mins. Transfer the eggs into a bowl and cover with ice-cold water. Peel and halve each egg.
5 Remove the chicken from the pan. Leave the sauce simmering and reducing with the lid off for 10-15 mins.
6 Pick the chicken meat and shred it. Add back to the sauce, stir and remove from the heat. Season and add more soy sauce and vinegar if needed.
7 Mix salad leaves with the peas and carrot. Place the salad on a plate, arrange the potatoes and chicken over the top then add the eggs.
British Lion Eggs www.eggrecipes.co.uk

12 SUNDAY

13 MONDAY

14 TUESDAY

15 WEDNESDAY

16 THURSDAY

17 FRIDAY

18 SATURDAY

A magical memory

CAUGHT RED-HANDED

As a young lad, I used to liberate fruit from the owner's tree without permission, otherwise known as scrumping for apples. When a group of us noticed some lovely apples in a garden, I volunteered to climb over the wall. As I reached my hand out to pick a large apple, there was a commotion and I saw a large dog bounding towards me, followed by a hostile-looking man waving a stick.

I scampered back to the wall and when I was halfway over it, I felt the dog's teeth on my ankle, but I still managed to make my escape. When I arrived home there was blood on my sock. My mother treated the wound which I told her was a cut from a piece of broken glass.

Then, there was a knock on the door and when my father answered it there was a policeman standing outside! He came in, gave me a verbal caution, and put the fear of God into me. Needless to say, I never went scrumping for apples again.
Peter Greenhalgh, Rugeley

Who am I?

Well known for my friendship with Frank Sinatra and Sammy Davis Jr, I loved to croon. The variety comedy series in my name ran for nine years but before that I was one half of a popular comedy duo.

Dean Martin

Nature diary

Go apple picking

Whether you want to make delicious apple crumble or apple sauce for the Sunday roast, now is a great time to head to your local orchard and pick fresh apples. To find your nearest orchard visit **www.pickyourownfarms.org.uk.**

Make life easy

Pop a marshmallow in the bottom of an ice cream cone before adding the ice cream. It will cleverly prevent the ice cream dripping out the bottom and ruining your outfit, plus gives a tasty treat to enjoy at the end.

Quirky Britain

Gurning is a British word meaning to pull a funny facial expression. Each summer, the **World Gurning Championships** sets out to crown a contestant who can pull the strangest face of all. The contest takes place every year in Egremont, Cumbria, as part of the town's Crab Fair, which dates back to 1267.

Recipe of the week

CHICKEN AND CAVOLO NERO TAGINE

SERVES: 4 PREP: 10 MINS COOK: 35 MINS

2 tbsp olive oil
200g (7oz) skinless chicken breast, cut into cubes
1 onion, finely diced
2 cloves garlic, crushed
1 tsp ground cinnamon
2 tsp ground cumin
2 tsp ground coriander
2 tsp paprika
½ tsp chilli flakes
200g (7oz) carrots, cubed
250g (9oz) butternut squash, cubed
400g (14oz) can chopped tomatoes
1 vegetable or chicken stock cube
400g (14oz) can chickpeas
50g (2oz) dried apricots, chopped
100g (3½oz) cavolo nero, sliced
200g (7oz) couscous
Fresh coriander

1 Heat the oil in a tagine or heavy-based flameproof casserole dish.
2 Fry the chicken for 2-3 mins, then remove from the dish and set aside. Add the onion to the dish and cook for 5 mins, then add the garlic and spices. Stir for 1 minute.
3 Add the chicken back in, then the carrots and butternut squash. Stir for 1 min then add the chopped tomatoes, a can full of water and the stock cube.
4 Leave to simmer for 15-20 mins, until the squash and carrots are soft.
5 Drain and rinse the chickpeas. Add these, the dried apricots and cavolo nero to the dish and simmer for another 5-10 mins.
6 Season to taste. Serve with couscous and fresh coriander.
www.discovergreatveg.co.uk

19 SUNDAY

20 MONDAY

21 TUESDAY

22 WEDNESDAY

23 THURSDAY

24 FRIDAY

25 SATURDAY

A magical memory

THE BEST OF TIMES

This poem was inspired by my Scottish mother who incredibly managed to raise ten children:

I often now can see her
With her merry twinkling eyes,
Washing, ironing, baking, sewing,
Making steak-and-kidney pies.
We never did go hungry,
She kept us all well fed,
Although we all had work to do
To earn our daily bread.
She'd tuck us up in bed at night
Then tell us all a story,
Wondrous tales of long ago
And Jesus and his glory.
We didn't have a lot of money,
But happiness and health,
Two loving parents, a cosy home,
Indeed, this was our wealth.

Jean Murphy, Somerset

Who am I?

I had 20 years in Hollywood starring alongside the likes of James Stewart, Cary Grant and Clark Gable. But eventually I gave it up to pursue my secret love to care for animals by setting up several charitable sanctuaries.

Doris Day

Nature diary

Plant dwarf iris bulbs in the home

Choose a shallow pot with drainage holes. Plant the bulbs 2-3 inches deep, side-by-side, pointed end up. Cover and water and move to a dark, cool location for 8 weeks. When the shoots reach 2 inches, move to a sunny spot, watering regularly.

Make life easy

Use a pizza wheel cutter to trim your herbs. Simply bunch them together on a chopping board and roll the cutter over them until finely sliced to the size you need for the recipe. Pizza wheels are also handy for cutting toast, peppers, cucumber and celery.

Quirky Britain

On the second to last weekend in September, the **Llandovery Sheep Festival** takes place on the edge of the Brecon Beacons, involving sheep dog trials to live sheep shearing. Its highlight is the race - a crazy sprint along the high street with teams racing fake sheep on wheels to the Market Square.

Recipe of the week

MEXICAN PULLED CHICKEN WRAPS WITH RADISH AND AVOCADO SALSA

SERVES: 2 PREP: 10 MINS COOK: 25 MINS

4 small chicken thighs
2 tsp ground cumin
2 tsp sweet smoked paprika
1 tbsp olive oil
Salt and pepper
1 avocado, sliced
15 mixed radishes, quartered
Small bunch coriander
½ lime
1 tsp olive oil
4 small tortilla wraps (corn if available)

1 Preheat the oven to 200°C/400°F /Gas Mark 6.
2 Place the chicken thighs in a bowl and add the ground cumin, sweet smoked paprika and olive oil, along with a pinch of salt and pepper. Mix well until the chicken is well coated.
3 Place the chicken thighs on a baking tray and bake in the oven for 20-25 mins, until cooked through and the juices run clear. Put to one side to cool, while you prepare the other ingredients.
4 Warm the tortillas in a dry frying pan and peel and slice the avocado.
5 Once the chicken has cooled, shred the meat off the bones and stir through any juices from the baking tray.
6 Serve the chicken in a warm tortilla, topped with the avocado, radishes, coriander and a squeeze of lime juice.
www.loveradish.co.uk

26 SUNDAY

27 MONDAY

28 TUESDAY

29 WEDNESDAY

30 THURSDAY

1 FRIDAY

2 SATURDAY

A magical memory

CARRY ON CAMPING

In 1962, aged 19, I was a staff driver in the WRAC when I went on a camping holiday to the Isles of Scilly with my friends, Sheelagh and Pauline. We had no tent or other equipment so we had to hire it all before we set off.

After a choppy crossing, we arrived on the island of St Mary and made our way to the campsite which was a farmer's field behind the Star Castle hotel. It was raining and after unpacking our equipment, it became clear that none of us had any idea of how to put up a tent. In the end, the farmer did it for us.

We finally got ourselves sorted and went to find the facilities which turned out to be a wooden bucket with a lid, plus a standpipe for water. Even so, we did pretty well - heads turned to see us emerging from our small tent, dressed up to the nines complete with bouffant hairstyles, ready to wander down to the Mermaid Inn to listen to the fishermen singing old sea shanties.

In the photo of me and Sheelagh, I am the one with a saucepan on my head!
Pat Rogers, Keighley

Who am I?

Born on a US military base in Germany, I had a habit of dying hard. I also played Harry S Stamper who gave up his life to save planet Earth when it was facing the end of the world.

Bruce Willis

Nature diary

Help hedgehogs

As our hedgehog friends return to hibernation, put out wet dog or cat food for them to munch on. Also consider making a hedgehog hole (about 13cm x 13cm) in the bottom of your garden fence so they can easily get around the neighbourhood.

Make life easy

Tumble-dryer sheets make great dusting cloths and even leave behind a residue which will help repel dust to save you on housework in the future. Use them to spruce up Venetian blinds, furniture and even your electrical goods.

Quirky Britain

Up to 350 competitors flock to Easdale Island, near Oban in Argyll, Scotland, for the **World Stone Skimming Championships**, on the last Sunday of September. Only naturally formed stones made of Easdale slate can be used which need to bounce at least twice for your go to be deemed a valid skim.

Recipe of the week

BROCCOLI AND TOFU MISO BROTH

SERVES: 2 PREP: 10 MINS COOK: 15 MINS

200g (7oz) Tenderstem broccoli
2 tbsp sesame oil
2 tbsp ginger, minced
1 medium red chilli, deseeded and finely chopped
½ block of firm tofu, cut into 1cm cubes
120g (4½oz) shiitake mushrooms, sliced
1ltr reduced-salt hot vegetable stock
2 tbsp reduced-salt light soy sauce
1 tbsp miso paste
1 tbsp rice wine vinegar
2 tbsp maple syrup
Handful pak choi leaves
Fresh red chilli, sliced
Spring onions, sliced thinly on an angle
1 tbsp sesame seeds
Fresh coriander, chopped

1 Preheat a griddle pan over a high heat and add a touch of oil. Grill the broccoli until charred (around 2 mins). Once cooked set aside.
2 Preheat a large wok or saucepan over a high heat. Add the sesame oil. When the pan is very hot and almost smoking throw in the ginger and chilli. Sauté for 1 minute before adding the tofu and mushrooms.
3 Toss and stir the mixture while cooking for 2 mins. Cook on high heat for 30 more seconds.
4 Turn the heat down low and add the vegetable stock, soy sauce, miso, rice wine vinegar and maple syrup. Simmer for 5 mins.
5 Just before removing from the heat, throw in the pak choi and grilled broccoli. Remove from the heat once the pak choi is slightly wilted
6 Top with the chilli, spring onion, sesame seeds and coriander.

www.tenderstem.co.uk

3 SUNDAY

4 MONDAY

5 TUESDAY

6 WEDNESDAY

7 THURSDAY

8 FRIDAY

9 SATURDAY

A magical memory

A REAL BOBBY-DAZZLER

Things have changed since I started using make-up in the Fifties. I liked Max Factor as it was the brand the Hollywood stars used and they all looked so glamorous in those days. My first lipsticks were a Christmas present from my auntie. One was a fuchsia colour by Outdoor Girl and the other was by Helena Rubinstein (I forget the shade). Cosmetic toothpaste had the effect of darkening one's gums to make teeth look whiter. I well remember the mascara that came in a black block with a little brush. I also wore false eyelashes which gave one a sultry look!

I still use the powder compact that I bought as a present for my mum. She used to have a little block of red rouge with a small puff to apply it and she always wore Evening in Paris perfume that came in a dark blue bottle. Now in my 70s, I am still battling on, trying to keep up with the latest fashion. I've been called a glamour puss and a bobby-dazzler in my time, so I feel I haven't done too badly!

The photo is of me with my daughter Jacqueline and son Alastair.
Sheila Davies, Wrexham

Who am I?

My elfish haircut, wide eyes, androgynous shape and endless legs put me on the cover of almost every magazine in the swinging Sixties. Today, I prove you can still be a glamorous model as well as being a gran.

Twiggy

Nature diary

Get rid of mushrooms

It's peak time for unwanted mushrooms popping up on your lawn. Reduce the chances of these growing by keeping your lawn free of leaves, watering your grass sparingly and by picking the mushrooms before they get too big.

Make life easy

Spiders invading your home? Discourage them with these clever natural deterrents. Place conkers on your window ledges and in your room corners, spiders hate them! And they don't like the smell of peppermint oil, so soak cotton balls in it and place near skirting boards or wherever you think they're getting in.

Quirky Britain

Rising from the water like rusty alien invaders from HG Wells' The War of the Worlds, the **Maunsell Army Forts** in the Thames Estuary are decaying reminders of our national defences in the Second World War. They can be seen by boat or, on a clear day, from Shoeburyness East Beach near Southend-on-Sea in Essex.

Recipe of the week

DATE AND WALNUT CAKE

SERVES: 8 PREP: 153 MINS COOK: 55-60 MINS

200g (7oz) stoned dates
150ml (¼pt) water
½ tsp bicarbonate of soda
3 eggs
100g (3½oz) brown sugar
100g (4fl oz) sunflower oil
200g (7oz) Doves Farm Organic Self Raising Wholemeal Flour
50g (2oz) chopped walnuts
Icing sugar

1 Preheat the oven to 180°C/350°F/Gas Mark 4.
2 Line a 20cm round deep, loose-bottomed cake tin with parchment paper.
3 Put the dates and water into a saucepan and bring slowly to the boil. Remove from the heat, stir in the bicarbonate of soda and leave to cool.
4 Break the eggs into a mixing bowl, add the sugar and beat together until light and airy.
5 Mix in the oil followed by the self-raising flour. Then stir in the date mixture and walnuts.
6 Tip the mixture into your prepared cake tin and smooth the top. Bake for 55-60 mins.
7 Allow to cool in the tin for 20 mins, before turning out onto a wire rack. Once completely cool, sieve over a little icing sugar before serving.

www.dovesfarm.co.uk

10 SUNDAY

11 MONDAY

12 TUESDAY

13 WEDNESDAY

14 THURSDAY

15 FRIDAY

16 SATURDAY

A magical memory

A GRAMMAR SCHOOL GIRL

There were times when I was a huge disappointment to my mum and the first time was in 1962 when I passed the Eleven Plus. Any other mother would have been proud and delighted, but not mine! Her philosophy was that hard work got you everything you needed in life and that higher education was a complete waste of time.

However, Dad put his foot down in my favour so when the long list of uniform and equipment required by Newquay Grammar School arrived, off we went (reluctantly) to Foster Triniman in East Street. Mum had always made my clothes and knitted my jumpers so having to buy these items from the specialist outfitter mortified her. Purchasing a hockey stick was the last straw and she positively refused when it came to the lacrosse stick, which was just as well as I never did get the hang of that game.

She got her own back by giving me a viciously tight home perm. Nobody spoke to me for the first two weeks of term until the overpowering fumes of Twink lotion were finally dispelled!
Denise Jones, Southport

Who am I?

My dark glasses were my trademark, along with a voice that could reach the highest notes. In the Sixties I had hit after hit, until I was affected by personal tragedies. Later, I teamed up with pals for a supergroup.

Roy Orbison

Nature diary

Cutting hedge appeal

Now is a great time to trim back your hedges with shears so they are crisp and tidy for the cold months ahead. Sharp edges will look very impressive when that first frost of winter comes and help them flourish come spring.

Make life easy

Just can't get that knot out of your favourite necklace? Sprinkle baby powder over it. Gently rub in the powder, then use a pin to pull apart the tangles. Once it's unknotted, simply clean off the baby powder in diluted soapy water.

Quirky Britain

Sharpen up! If you've always loved the smell of pencil shavings, you're sure to see the point (!) of the **Derwent Pencil Museum in Keswick**. You'll be 'lead' through a replica graphite mine to see the longest pencil in the world, Second World War pencils with hidden maps and lots more.

Recipe of the week

SWEET POTATO JACKETS WITH WATERCRESS, TAHINI SAUCE AND ROASTED CHICKPEAS

SERVES: 4 PREP: 10 MINS COOK: 45 MINS
4 sweet potatoes
400g (14oz) tin chickpeas
2 tsp smoked paprika
Salt and pepper
30ml (1fl oz) olive oil
85g (3oz) watercress
Zest and juice of 1 lemon
60g (2½oz) Greek yogurt
2 tbsp tahini
Seeds of one pomegranate

1 Preheat the oven to 180°C/350°F/Gas Mark 4.
2 Wrap each potato in foil and place onto a large baking sheet. Bake for roughly 45 mins depending on the size of the potatoes, checking that the centre is soft.
3 While the potatoes are cooking, drain and rinse the chickpeas. Tip them into a baking tray and sprinkle with the smoked paprika and a pinch of salt. Drizzle with the olive oil and place in the oven for 8-10 mins, or until crispy. Remove from the oven, stir in the watercress and allow to wilt.
4 Whisk together the lemon juice and zest, yogurt and tahini. Season to taste. Split the sweet potatoes lengthways then fill with the chickpea and watercress mixture. Drizzle over the tahini sauce and sprinkle with pomegranate seeds to finish.

www.watercress.co.uk

17 SUNDAY

18 MONDAY

19 TUESDAY

20 WEDNESDAY

21 THURSDAY

22 FRIDAY

23 SATURDAY

A magical memory

THE GRANDEST GRAN OF ALL

This photo of my nan was taken on the day we entered her for the Grandest Grandmother competition when we were all on a caravan holiday in Hemsby in 1993. We decorated her wheelchair for the occasion and added the 'Ratty' labels as that was the nickname my husband had given her.

Needless to say, she won and the prize was another week in Hemsby where she was the life and soul of the camp. She proudly displayed her trophy and told everyone about our extra week's holiday.

When I was growing up, she played a big part in our lives. I enjoyed nothing more than listening to her stories of the old days over a cup of tea. If life was difficult, she faced it with a smile on her face and would do anything for anyone. When she was no longer able to live on her own she moved in with my parents and it was wonderful to have her in the midst of our family life. It was an honour to be her granddaughter and we still talk about her every single day.
Nicola Hunt, Hornchurch

Who am I?

Starting in The Belles of St Trinian's, I became a household name by enthusiastically exercising in a bikini alongside Kenneth Williams. Later into my career, you'd know it was me when you heard someone yelling, "get out of my pub".

Barbara Windsor

Nature diary

Autumn leaves

Raking up the leaves from the garden, especially if you have a lots of trees, can feel like a chore, but rather than raking, mow them. The lawn mower will break them up while broken-down leaves will provide the soil with nutrients.

Make life easy

Toothpaste is your shoe cleaning essential! Use it on leather shoes by rubbing a little into any scuffs using a soft cloth and use to clean the white rubber part of your trainers. Wipe away with a damp cloth and they'll be as good as new. Cheaper than buying a special product and does the same job!

Quirky Britain

This giant wooden treehouse in **Alnwick Garden, Northumberland**, looks like something from the pages of a fairytale, with its wooden walkways and suspension bridges. But this quirky structure actually houses a fully functioning restaurant which feels just as magical on the inside, featuring twinkling lights and roaring log fire.

Recipe of the week

BRIOCHE LATTE FRENCH TOAST WITH STRAWBERRIES

SERVES: 4 PREP: 10 MINS COOK: 15 MINS

4 eggs
1 x 330ml carton of Arctic Iced Coffee Latte
8 slices of brioche
Strawberries
Maple syrup

1 In a bowl beat the eggs with the Arctic Iced Coffee.
2 Soak the slices of brioche in the egg mixture until they have all soaked up the liquid.
3 Heat a frying pan and fry each slice in butter until golden, around 3 mins each side.
4 Serve on a place with chopped strawberries and a drizzle of maple syrup.
www.arcticicedcoffee.co.uk

24 SUNDAY

25 MONDAY

26 TUESDAY

27 WEDNESDAY

28 THURSDAY

29 FRIDAY

30 SATURDAY

A magical memory

EEE, IT'S OUR ELSIE

This group photo was taken at my cousin Daphne Cherry's wedding in October 1962. That's me in the front wearing a green coat – I didn't realise the bottom button was undone.

The lady peeping over my shoulder is my aunt Jess who had exclaimed as we arrived at the church: "Elsie Tanner!" As my husband Tom and I didn't have a television set at that time, I didn't know what she meant until she explained that she thought I looked like Pat Phoenix, the actress who played the temptress of Coronation Street.

I had worn my hair in that style for some time, but nobody in the office had ever commented on it. I later learned that Pat Phoenix was a redhead while I was a brunette.

Over the years, I've shown this picture to various people and asked them if they recognised anyone. They all say: "Oh, that's Elsie Tanner. How do you know her?" which just goes to show that I don't look like her anymore. And I'm not aged 20 now, either!
Yvonne Parsons, Exmouth

Who am I?

Born in Swansea, I was the darling of British television before being cast in The Mask of Zorro in 1998. Marrying into acting royalty, I later won myself a BAFTA for a murderously good part in the film musical Chicago.

Catherine Zeta-Jones

Nature diary

Blackbird beauties

Noticed a big boom in blackbirds? Their numbers increase in autumn as many European birds come here for winter for the milder conditions. Like other thrushes, blackbirds feed on windfall apples in gardens so don't tidy them all away.

Make life easy

Rescue an overly acidic tomato pasta sauce by adding diced onion (fried off first) and half a teaspoon of sugar. Grated carrot is another good option, or you could try the traditional Italian method and allow your sauce to gently simmer for 3-4 hours to make a delicious flavour.

Quirky Britain

Go back to the pantry of yesteryear with a trip to the **Museum of Brands, Packaging and Advertising,** in London - the only museum of its kind in the world. See all the products you remember from growing up and long before, such as First World War Oxo cubes, Thirties' KitKats and a Seventies' Chopper bike.

Recipe of the week

SEAFOOD AND BROCCOLI PIE

SERVES: 6 PREP: 15 MINS COOK: 45 MINS

40g (1½oz) butter
1 medium onion, chopped
40g (1½oz) flour
150ml (¼pt) white wine
300ml (10fl oz) semi-skimmed milk
200g (7oz) Tenderstem broccoli
500g (1lb 2oz) skinless salmon fillet, cut into 3cm cubes
200g (7oz) raw peeled tiger prawns
3 eggs, hard boiled and chopped
1 tbsp chopped dill or parsley
For the mashed potato topping:
900g (2lb) potatoes
4 tbsp semi skimmed milk
10g (½oz) butter
25g (1oz) cheddar, grated

1 Preheat the oven to 200°C/400°F /Gas Mark 6.
2 Melt the butter in a large saucepan and sauté the onion with the bay leaf until softened. Stir in the flour for 30 seconds before gradually adding the wine. Keep stirring to prevent lumps, before doing the same with the milk. Bring to a simmer and cook for a few mins until you have a thick sauce.
3 Cut the broccoli into bite-size pieces and stir into the sauce. Simmer for 5 mins.
4 Stir in the salmon and prawns, then simmer for a few mins, until the prawns are pink. Add the eggs, dill or parsley and season to taste. Spoon into a large ovenproof dish.
5 Meanwhile, make the mash. Boil potatoes until tender. Drain and mash with milk and butter.
6 Spread the mash over the filling. Scatter over the cheese. Place in the oven for 30-40 mins until the topping is golden.
www.tenderstem.co.uk

31 SUNDAY

1 MONDAY

2 TUESDAY

3 WEDNESDAY

4 THURSDAY

5 FRIDAY

6 SATURDAY

A magical memory

AWAY FROM HOME

As our home town of Plymouth was a target for the Luftwaffe during the war, my sister and I were evacuated to safer parts of Devon. Our first billet was a farm, but as town children we had no idea of rural life. When the farmer's wife sent me to collect eggs from the hen coop I did as I was told. Nobody said not to collect the china eggs in the house as well. One morning after breakfast we were told to put our coats on, then we noticed our suitcases by the front door. We were being moved on...

Our next billet was with a lady who was not too keen on having evacuees and we were made to feel we were a nuisance. She frightened us when she walked around at night with a lighted candle that cast big black shadows on the wall.

When our parents came to visit, I ran down the hill to greet them at the railway station. I remember the disbelief on my mother's face as she asked: "Why is your hair such a mess? Haven't you got a comb?" Fortunately, the bombing had become less intense so our parents felt able to take us home with them.
Louise Childs, Newton Abbot

Who am I?

Having started life as a welder in the Glasgow shipyards, I went onto star in The Secret Policeman's Ball, Mrs Brown and The Man Who Sued God. A comedian and actor, I'm known in my homeland as The Big Yin.

Billy Connolly

Nature diary

Pumpkin pots

Use leftover pumpkins from Hallowe'en to make seasonal plant pots. Simply cut off the top of your pumpkin, scrape out the insides to make a plant pot shape and place inside a small potted plant.

Make life easy

Fed up with the never-ending chore of ironing bedding and shirts? Add a few ice-cubes or a wet cloth to your dryer along with your wrinkled items. The ice melts and turns to steam, helping to remove the creases in a jiffy – you can put your ironing board away!

Quirky Britain

Also known as the **Quay House of Conwy**, the self-proclaimed **'Smallest House in Great Britain'** is a one up, one down cottage measuring just 72 inches across, 122 inches high and 120 inches deep. The building was lived in until May 1900 when it was condemned as being unfit for human habitation.

Recipe of the week

BAKED PUMPKIN AND WATERCRESS FONDUE

SERVES: 2-4 PREP: 15 MINS COOK: 1 HOUR 30 MINS

1 small pumpkin
150g (5oz) grated mature cheddar
150g (5oz) grated gruyère
150g (5oz) grated emmental
30g (1oz) watercress, roughly chopped
25g (1oz) plain flour (or use cornflour for gluten free)
50ml (2fl oz) dry white wine
150g (5oz) crème fraîche
2 small shallots, finely diced
1 garlic clove, finely chopped
Black pepper

1 Preheat the oven to 170°C/325°F/Gas Mark 3.
2 Take a sharp knife and carefully remove the 'lid' of the pumpkin, keeping to one side. Scoop out the seeds and stringy insides, leaving the edible flesh intact. Put the lid back on the pumpkin and place onto an oven tray.
3 Roast for around 45 mins, or until the flesh is just cooked through. Remove from the oven and allow to cool while you make the fondue mixture.
4 Add the grated cheese, watercress and plain flour to a mixing bowl. Mix thoroughly so that the cheese and watercress are evenly coated with a fine layer of flour. In a separate bowl, mix together the white wine, crème fraiche, shallots and garlic. Pepper to taste. Combine the cheese mixture and the crème fraîche, then fill up the pumpkin.
5 Put the pumpkin back into the oven for 30 mins, or until the cheese is melted and bubbling. Serve with bread, more watercress, or roasted vegetables for dunking.
www.watercress.co.uk

7 SUNDAY

8 MONDAY

9 TUESDAY

10 WEDNESDAY

11 THURSDAY

12 FRIDAY

13 SATURDAY

A magical memory

MY LOVING FOSTER MOTHER

This photo of me with my foster mother, Daphne, and her two sons, David and Jonathan, was taken on her 70th birthday. Ten years later, we were all together again to celebrate her 80th birthday.

I was fostered by Daphne in the early Seventies and was with the family for two years. She already had David and while I was there she gave birth to Jonathan. I used to help out with the baby and she taught me how to cook and how to keep house, all the skills that came in useful later in my own life. I was so grateful to her for taking me on as not everyone wanted to foster a teenager at that time.

When my husband and I were invited to Daphne's 70th birthday, her sons were really pleased to see me and it was nice to be remembered. At the next party, in 2018, a lady sitting next to me asked me how I knew Daphne. When I told her that she had been my foster mother when I was 16 she was taken aback by how long we had stayed in contact, catching up three or four times a year.
Lynda Crossland, Hampshire

Who am I?

Born Virginia Katherine McMath, I'm one half of the greatest dance double acts. Ostrich feathers became me as I glided face-to-face with my partner. I always said I did the same as him, just backwards and in heels.

Ginger Rogers

Nature diary

Tulip time

Now's the time to plant tulip bulbs for next spring. Find a sunny spot in your garden with well-draining soil. Plant bulbs 4-6 inches apart and at least 8 inches deep, setting the bulb with the pointy end up. Water straight after planting.

Make life easy

Freshen up your carpets and rugs with baking soda. Vacuum the area first, then sparingly sprinkle over the baking soda using a flour shaker. Leave for an hour or two before vacuuming again. Make sure you empty your vacuum straight afterwards and clean the filte, then enjoy those pristine and sweet-smelling carpets.

Quirky Britain

The Yorkshire Dales is home to the **Oldest Sweet Shop in England,** in Pateley Bridge. Row upon row of glass jars are filled with handmade traditional sweets weighed out by the quarter of a pound into old-fashioned scales. The building itself dates back to the 17th Century with original features, fixtures and fittings.

Recipe of the week

BOOZY HAZELNUT HOT CHOCOLATE

SERVES: 2 PREP: 5 MINS COOK: 5 MINS

500ml (1pt) hazelnut milk
4 tbsp cacao powder
2 tbsp maple syrup
30g (1oz) dark chocolate (we used 70 per cent)
4 tbsp Frangelico hazelnut liqueur
Handful of marshmallows

1 Place the hazelnut milk into a small saucepan over a low heat for a few mins until steaming. Add the squares of dark chocolate and stir, but do not let the milk boil. Remove from the heat.
2 In each cup, mix 2 tbsp cacao powder, 1 tbsp maple syrup and 2 tbsp Frangelico and stir to form a paste.
3 Divide the hot hazelnut milk between each mug and stir well.
4 Serve with some marshmallows on top and a stick of dark chocolate if you're feeling extra indulgent.
Annabel Wray and Victoria Knight, professional chefs and co-founders of Hakuna Foods

14 SUNDAY

15 MONDAY

16 TUESDAY

17 WEDNESDAY

18 THURSDAY

19 FRIDAY

20 SATURDAY

A magical memory

YOU'RE DOIN' FINE, OKLAHOMA

I loved dressing up my dolls and teddies in various outfits when I was a child. The teddy bear sitting on my lap was called Okla, presumably inspired by my nan's favourite musical, Oklahoma. I idolised Okla even though he was secondhand, having been given to me when I was two by a family friend.

I must have been about 16 when Mother decided he was getting a bit the worse for wear and put him out with the rubbish. My dad, who wasn't usually sentimental, saw Okla's head poking out of the dustbin and rescued him, scolding my mother for her cruelty. In an effort to be forgiven, she sewed some new pads onto Okla's paws and replaced his eyes. This wasn't good from a collector's point of view, but by then Okla wasn't going anywhere. Dad made sure he had a permanent home with us.

Once upon a time Okla used to growl like a bear if you pressed his tummy, but he has been silent for years. He is still with me, though, and at 65-plus is happily retired.
Linda Kettle, Portsmouth

Who am I?

Brother of a famous director and actor, I'm best known for my love of the planet and its wildlife. Widely considered a national treasure - although I'm not keen on the title myself - I used to be the controller of BBC 2.
David Attenborough

Nature diary

Mistletoe moments

Have a look for the first signs of some festive greenery as mistletoe makes its move. You'll find it growing in the branches of hawthorn, poplar, lime and apple trees in gardens, orchards, parklands and even churchyards.

Make life easy

Make light work of halving cherry tomatoes by placing them all on a plate and then placing another plate on top. Using a large and sharp knife carefully slide it in the horizontal gap between the two plates and you'll halve them all in one swift go.

Quirky Britain

The medieval village of **Lavenham** in Suffolk is one of the quirkiest villages in the UK, with half-timbered Tudor houses are painted in rich colours and are so crooked that they look as though they are learning on each other. It's believed that their distorted appearance inspired the poem, 'A Crooked Little Man'.

Recipe of the week

SPICED APPLE PORRIDGE

SERVES: 2 PREP: 5 MINS COOK: 5 MINS

2 Pink Lady apples
500ml (1pt) soya or almond milk
85g (3oz) porridge oats
1 tbsp mixed seeds, plus extra to garnish
1 tbsp coconut sugar (optional)
1 tsp cinnamon
½ tsp ginger
¼ tsp nutmeg
Pinch cloves
To serve:
Maple syrup & cashew nut butter

1 Core and chop one of the apples (thinly slice the other and set aside). Add the chopped apple to a pan with the rest of the ingredients.
2 Simmer and cook over a medium heat for 5-7 mins.
3 Pour into two bowls and top each with some of the finely sliced apple, a sprinkle of mixed seeds, a dash of maple syrup and a drizzle of cashew nut butter.

www.pinkladyapples.co.uk

21 SUNDAY

22 MONDAY

23 TUESDAY

24 WEDNESDAY

25 THURSDAY

26 FRIDAY

27 SATURDAY

A magical memory

A SIGN OF THE TIMES

Here I am (on the right) with my mother,
Ruby, who used to have a greengrocer's shop
in Manor Park in East London. It was open
every day except Sunday which was a half day.
The sign on the front, R Clarke, Fruiterer and
Greengrocer, needed to be repainted every few
years. The elderly man who came to do this
was a wonderful artist who always asked for
'a spot of cash for me lunch'. On his return, he
would slowly climb the ladder, wobbling as he
went. He never fell and his painting was even
better after his liquid lunch.

Mum was renowned for her beetroot which
she cooked in a room behind the shop in a large
bread bin over two gas burners. She used to
say: "I'm not much of a cook, but I can certainly
cook bloody beetroot!". I think she felt a bit
naughty saying 'bloody'.

In the summer, Mum brought home
any strawberries that she couldn't sell.
There was only the two of us to eat them
as the neighbours got tired of being asked
if they'd like them for free. To this day, I
hate strawberries, strawberry jam and even
strawberry ice-cream!
Alexandra Hatch, Essex

Who am I?

Born in Hawaii in 1945, I'm known to fans as
The Divine Miss M. Starring in The Rose in
1979 I also appeared in Hocus Pocus, The First
Wives Club and lately played the leading lady
in Broadway's Hello Dolly.

Bette Midler

Nature diary

Plant narcissi

Narcissi are great to plant inside if you don't feel like heading into the cold. Place a layer of pebbles in a container and arrange the bulbs on top, placing pebbles around to stabilise them. Water and leave in a sunny spot.

Make life easy

Clean dirty or misty car headlights using a clean, dry cloth and a little toothpaste. Rubbing it into your headlights will not only make them sparkle, but will also help prevent them fogging up, which is handy as the winter nights start to draw in.

Quirky Britain

Delve down beneath the streets of London into the former engineering depot of Mail Rail at **The Postal Museum**. See and hear all about the people who worked there and experience their lives below ground. Alongside exhibition galleries, visitors can also hop on a train and take a subterranean ride through some of the original tunnels.

Recipe of the week

ROASTED PARSNIP AND CARROT SOUP WITH KALE CRISPS

SERVES: 4-6 PREP: 15 MINS COOK: 40 MINS

500g (1lb 2oz) parsnips, peeled and cut into 3cm chunks
300g (10½oz) carrots, peeled and cut into 3cm chunks
1 tbsp maple syrup
3 tbsp olive oil
150g (5oz) pack kale, stalks and leaves separated
2 onions, roughly chopped
2 garlic cloves, crushed
Pinch of salt
2 tsp ground cumin
500ml (1pt) fresh vegetable stock
1-2 tbsp lemon juice
4 tbsp yogurt (non-dairy if desired)
Black pepper

1 Preheat oven to 200°C/400°F/Gas Mark 6.
2 Toss parsnips and carrots with maple syrup and 1 tbsp oil. Add to a lined baking tray, season and roast for 20 mins.
3 Heat 1 tbsp oil in saucepan over a medium heat. Chop the kale stalks, then add to the pan with the onions, garlic and salt. Cover with lid and cook for 12 mins, stirring occasionally. Remove the lid, add the cumin and cook for 3 mins. Add roasted parsnips and carrots, stock and 750ml (1¼pt) water. Boil then simmer for 10 mins.
4 Turn the oven down to 170°C/325F/Gas Mark 3. Tear the kale leaves into 4-5cm pieces. Toss with the remaining oil and a few drops of lemon juice. Season and roast on a baking tray for 12-15 mins, turning halfway.
5 Blend the soup with 1 tbsp lemon juice until smooth. Add a splash of water to loosen if needed, then reheat. To serve, swirl in yogurt and top with the kale leaf crisps and black pepper.

www.waitrose.com/recipe

28 SUNDAY

29 MONDAY

30 TUESDAY

1 WEDNESDAY

2 THURSDAY

3 FRIDAY

4 SATURDAY

A magical memory

SEQUINS, SONGS AND SHOES

Our mum, Frances, was the best of mothers. She and Dad were married in 1934 and had four children. Mum made all our clothes, including the beautiful outfit she is wearing in this photo taken with my dad. She made ballgowns for a dance team known as Ernest Page and Dulcie Burton. All the sequins were sewn on by hand. She also cut Dad's hair and even sat on the kitchen floor to cobble his shoes, cutting the leather and edging it in wax. But the best thing of all was that she loved us with the fierceness of a lion protecting her cubs.

Mum sang opera beautifully as she did the washing. After the war, she became a Red Cross nurse and helped friends and neighbours to bring children into the world as well as laying out their dead.

The last thing she made was a beautiful crib and covers for my grandson. Although she didn't live to see him born, we knew she had wrapped him in her love.
Dorothy Corner, Bradford

Who am I?

My fame hit 'fever' pitch in the Seventies, cemented by a movie where quiffs and leather jackets were all the rage. After a few flops, in 1994 I made a comeback dancing the twist with Uma Thurman in a diner.

John Travolta

Nature diary

Repair damaged pots

A mild winter day is a good time to fix any damaged plant pots while they are not in use. Shallow exterior cracks can be fixed by applying a mixture of PVA glue and sand. And why not decorate your plant pots in time for spring next year?

Make life easy

Protect your potted plants from winter frost and prevent your pots from cracking by wrapping them in cardboard, bubble wrap or sacking material during the colder months. Stuff any gaps with straw, hay or compost to keep them snug ready for next year.

Quirky Britain

The city of **York** has a network of quirky narrow passages – also known as 'snickleways' – around every corner, which can only be travelled through by foot. As they are largely medieval, they often feature weird and wonderful names such Mad Alice Lane, Whip-Ma-Whop-Ma-Gate, Nether Hornpot Lane and Hole-in-the-Wall.

Recipe of the week

TRIFLE WITH BISCOFF MOUSSE AND RED FRUITS

SERVES: 6 PREP: 15 MINS COOK: 90 MINS

Cake:
120g (4½oz) butter, at room temperature
75g (3oz) light brown Demerara sugar
50g (2oz) sugar
3 eggs
75ml (2½fl oz) groundnut oil
75ml (2½fl oz) buttermilk
200g (7oz) self-raising flour
A pinch of salt
100g (3½oz) chocolate chips
Trifle:
150g (5oz) Lotus Biscoff biscuits
250ml (½pt) whipping cream
250g (9oz) mascarpone
1 bag of red fruit from the freezer
1 tbsp sugar

1 Preheat the oven to 170°C/325°F/Gas Mark 3.
2 Beat the butter, brown sugar and demerara sugar together until creamy. Add eggs one by one.
3 Add the oil and buttermilk. Mix thoroughly.
3 Sprinkle in flour and salt.
4 Line a baking sheet with baking paper (or use a rectangular baking tin, 40cm x 30cm) and add the mixture. Smooth the surface and sprinkle over chocolate chips.
5 Bake in the oven for 30 mins, then leave to cool.
6 Crumble the Biscoff and put in the cream to soften. Whip the cream when the Biscoff have absorbed all the cream. Fold in the mascarpone.
7 Make the fruit compote by heating the frozen fruit with the sugar and leaving to cool.
8 Use a small pastry cutter to cut circles out of the cake. Spoon some fruit compote into 6 glass dishes, place a circle of cake on top and cover with a layer of Biscoff mousse. Repeat these layers and finish with pieces of Biscoff.
www.lotusbiscoff.com

5 SUNDAY

6 MONDAY

7 TUESDAY

8 WEDNESDAY

9 THURSDAY

10 FRIDAY

11 SATURDAY

A magical memory

THE WINTER OF '63

Here I am aged five, wearing a jumper that my mother knitted for me. Later, when I was 16, I had a part-time job at a newsagent's in Bedfordshire. On Saturdays I served behind the counter and was a paper boy on Sundays. On this particular delivery day in 1963, I woke at six o'clock as usual and got myself ready for work. When I went to open the front door I was confronted by a four-foot high snowdrift.

I started walking to the paper shop which was six miles away. I didn't have a bike or wellies! The snow was at least three feet deep the whole way. By the time I reached the shop I was freezing cold, only to be greeted by the manager telling me that the parents of two of the other paper boys had phoned in to say they were sick so could I do the extra rounds.

It took me six hours, walking along the tops of garden walls to make sure the customers got their papers safe and dry. My reward was to take home fifteen shillings – five bob for each bag of papers delivered.
Colin Warby, King's Lynn

Who am I?

Some people call me a princess, but I'm just an ordinary girl from Pennsylvania who gained stardom in Mogambo alongside Clark Gable. You'd know me well for living it up in High Society and catching a thief for Alfred Hitchcock.

Grace Kelly

Nature diary

Hello holly!

Now is a great time to plant holly to use sprigs for your Christmas decorations next year! Dig a hole (60x60cm and 30cm deep). Add a layer of compost and place the roots in the hole so it is level with the soil surface. Fill in and water well.

Make life easy

Keep your home toasty and warm with the help of a handy kitchen essential. Simply cover a large piece of card with kitchen foil and then place it behind your radiator. This will help reflect the heat back into the room and could even save on energy bills.

Quirky Britain

There's nothing as British as a cup of tea - except perhaps a family-run museum celebrating teapots! **Teapot Island**, in Yalding, Kent, has more than 8,200 objects to browse (worth in excess of £120,000) including designs featuring Princess Diana, Doctor Who and Star Wars. They also have 'paint your own' pottery available to buy.

Recipe of the week

PECANS, PEAR, CHICORY AND STILTON SALAD

SERVES: 2 PREP: 20 MINS COOK: 5 MINS

50g (2oz) pecans
2 chicory heads
1 blush pear
½ a lemon
50g (2oz) Stilton cheese (or gorgonzola)
1 tsp chopped chives
Dressing
1 tbsp white balsamic vinegar
40ml (1½fl oz) olive oil
½ lemon, juice
½ tsp mustard
½ tsp honey
Salt and pepper

1 Preheat oven to 180°C/350°F/ Gas Mark 4.
2 Spread the pecans out on a baking sheet and bake for eight mins, until fragrant. Set aside to cool.
3 Make the vinaigrette by whisking all of the dressing ingredients together. Set aside.
4 Cut the base off each chicory head and gently pull off each leaf. Wash the leaves, dry, then place in a serving bowl. Drizzle a few tablespoons of dressing and toss the salad.
5 Chop the pecans into smaller pieces. Cut the pears into thin slices (unpeeled), discard the core. Squeeze a lemon onto the pear to stop it from turning brown, then scatter over the chicory. Crumble the stilton and scatter onto the salad, followed by the pecans and the chives.
6 Add extra dressing if required and serve.

Annabel Wray and Victoria Knight, professional chefs and co-founders of Hakuna Foods

13 SUNDAY

14 MONDAY

15 TUESDAY

16 WEDNESDAY

17 THURSDAY

18 FRIDAY

19 SATURDAY

A magical memory

PANTO TIME!

In the small town of Innerleithen in the Scottish Borders, the local Boy Scout troop had a tradition of putting on pantomimes. This photo was taken in 1958 when I was in the cast of Ali Baba. I am second from the right in the front row and next to me is my good friend, Gillian, who I still meet regularly.

It all started the year before when I was 15 and my boyfriend at the time persuaded me to audition for one of the female parts. I did, and I got the part of Lola in Robinson Crusoe which we performed in the town's Memorial Hall and the Chambers Institution in Peebles. After that, I was busy with exams and didn't perform in the next two pantos although I became friendly with the stage manager, John. Two years later we were engaged and married in 1964.

My love of singing and dancing has never left me and when we moved to Bathgate I joined the town's amateur dramatic society. I took part in various productions and John again acted as stage manager. This photo is a reminder of a happy time that changed the course of my life.

Margaret Samuel, West Lothian

Who am I?

Best known for my career in stand-up and television, I became the youngest ever host of the Royal Variety Show. You'd recognise my floppy hair or my skipping walk anywhere. I've also been a judge on Britain's Got Talent.

Michael McIntyre

Nature diary

Starling of wonder

Look up overhead at dusk for the truly magnificent sight of starling murmurations swirling overhead in unison. Gathering together to keep warm at night, they put on a spectacular show all over Britain.

Make life easy

Store rolls of wrapping paper in hanging garment bags to be placed either in the wardrobe or in under-the-bed storage boxes. Also include scissors, tape, tags and ribbons in the bags so everything is easily to hand whenever needed at Christmas and for birthdays.

Quirky Britain

The Forbidden Corner is a unique labyrinth of tunnels, chambers, follies and surprises created within a four-acre garden in the heart of Tupgill Park and the Yorkshire Dales. Visitors to the gardens are not provided with a map of any kind, but are instead given a checklist of places to be discovered.

Recipe of the week

FESTIVE GINGERBREAD

MAKES: 25 PREP: 20 MINS COOK: 10 MINS

125g (4½oz) Waitrose Essential Unsalted Butter
100g (3½oz) dark brown muscovado sugar
4 tbsp golden syrup
325g (11½oz) plain flour, plus extra for dusting
1 tsp bicarbonate of soda
2 tsp ground ginger
5 tbsp icing sugar
3 tbsp decorative sprinkles

1 Preheat the oven to 170°C/325°F/Gas Mark 3.
2 Line 2 large baking trays with baking parchment.
3 Melt the butter, sugar and syrup together in a saucepan, then remove from the heat.
4 Sieve the flour, bicarbonate of soda and ginger into a bowl, then stir in the melted ingredients to make a stiff dough. Turn out onto a lightly floured surface and roll to a thickness of about 5mm.
5 Stamp shapes out of the dough using Christmas cookie cutters or cut round festive templates.
6 Place onto the baking trays and bake (in batches) for 9-10 mins until golden brown.
7 Remove from the oven. While still warm use a skewer or chopstick to make holes to hang the biscuits on the tree. Leave to cool completely on a wire rack.
8 Mix the icing sugar with a splash of water to make thick icing, then drizzle over the biscuits and decorate with sprinkles.

www.waitrose.com/recipe

19 SUNDAY

20 MONDAY

21 TUESDAY

22 WEDNESDAY

23 THURSDAY

24 FRIDAY

25 SATURDAY

A magical memory

CHRISTMAS WITH GRANDMA

Here I am standing in the doorway of my grandmother's house in 1939. When I was growing up families lived close to each other, often in the same street. The companionship of family, friends and neighbours was more important than money.

Grandma's house was always open to anyone who needed help, to talk about their problems or to have a cup of tea and a singalong. My memory of Grandma is that she sorted everything out for everyone.

She was a nurse to anyone who was ill and looked after her own mother who lived in the next street and was bedridden. We did not run to the doctor in those days as we would have had to pay for treatment.

Christmas was a wonderful time at Grandma's house. She brought her tree out on December 1 and we helped to decorate it. She always managed to give her grandchildren a little present which was a real treat as it was often the only gift we got except perhaps an orange and an apple from Father Christmas. When she died at the age of 80, I was heartbroken.

Betty Wheeler, Doncaster

Who am I?

I got happy singing and dancing but having performed from the age of two - and making my big break at 13 - I didn't always have a merry little time of it. I'm best known for my adventures far from Kansas.

Judy Garland

Nature diary

Poinsettia pointers

Check your poinsettia's soil before buying it. The soil should be neither dripping wet nor totally dry. If it is, it's probably not been given the proper TLC it needs and isn't likely to last long when you get it home.

Make life easy

Not a fan of mushy Brussels sprouts? Don't bother scoring a cross on the bottom as it will make them get soggy quicker. Instead, trim the ends and remove any tatty leaves. Halve larger sprouts before cooking but leave smaller ones whole.

Quirky Britain

The Burning the Clocks event, held in Brighton, marks the shortest day of the year (December 21). Local people make their own paper and willow lanterns and, after parading through the city, pass them into a blazing bonfire on Brighton beach as a token of the year's end.

Recipe of the week

APPLE MINCE PIES

MAKES: 12 PREP: 30 MINS + CHILLING TIME
COOK: 20 MINS

1 x 375g (13oz) pack ready-rolled sweet shortcrust pastry
200g (7oz) mincemeat
1 Pink Lady Apple, cored and finely diced
25g (1oz) dried cranberries
Icing sugar to dust

1 Preheat the oven to 200°C/400°F/Gas Mark 6.
2 Unroll the pastry onto a clean board. Using a 7cm cutter stamp out 12 circles and use to line a bun tin. Put in the fridge for 30 mins. Reserve the pastry trimmings.
3 In a bowl mix together the mincemeat, diced apple and dried cranberries. Spoon a little of the apple mincemeat into each pastry case.
4 Using the pastry trimmings stamp out 12 small star or heart shapes. Put a star or heart on the top of each mincemeat tart. Bake in the oven for 15-20 mins until lightly golden and cooked.
5 Leave to cool for 5 mins then transfer to a wire rack and dust with icing sugar.
www.pinkladyapples.co.uk

26 SUNDAY

27 MONDAY

28 TUESDAY

29 WEDNESDAY

30 THURSDAY

31 FRIDAY

1 SATURDAY

A magical memory

TIDINGS OF GREAT JOY

This photo of my husband Bill and me holding up a cheque in front of our Christmas tree, was taken when I won first prize in a competition run by a slimming magazine. The winning slogan for Marvel dried milk was 'Slimline tastes mean Trimline waists'.

In addition to a cash prize of £1,500 I won a coffee set which I had to collect from the magazine's London office. My niece came with me on the train. We were sent enough money for first-class fares, but we travelled second class so we had some money to spend in the shops. The coffee set turned out to be in a very big box and after lunch in a bistro with the editor we took a taxi to catch the train home.

When we arrived at the station we found the drivers had gone on strike and when we eventually got a train, it was crowded. Luckily, we were offered seats - probably because of the large box we were carrying. No mobile phones so we couldn't let anyone know we'd be late and we finally arrived back at nine o'clock. That is the one and only time I have ever been to London.
Pat Mason, Skipton

Who am I?

With a career spanning over 60 wonderful years, I'm the third top-selling artist in UK Singles Chart history. Starting my career with a rock n roll backing group, it was taking a summer holiday that kickstarted my movie stardom.

Cliff Richard

Nature diary

Have a new year clean

During 'betwixtmas' why not take the chance to get your gardening tools in good order for the new year? Warm soapy water can be used to clean hand tools such as secateurs and spades; buff away rust spots with steel wool.

Make life easy

Keep your Christmas tree baubles safe and secure until next year by storing them in empty egg cartons before you put them away in the loft. Other handy festive storage ideas include storing bead garlands in empty drinks bottle containers and wrapping your tree lights around an old hose reel.

Quirky Britain

Travel back in time and discover what life was like in the North East England of yesteryear at the **Beamish Open-Air Museum**. Taste traditional food from a coal-fired range, hop on board a tram or steam train, play schoolyard games together and pop into the Co-op shops.

Recipe of the week

TURKEY, RED LENTIL AND SPINACH CURRY

SERVES: 4 PREP: 15 MINS COOK: 35 MINS

150g (5oz) red split lentils, rinsed
1 tbsp sunflower oil
1 onion, diced
1 tbsp fresh root ginger, grated
3 garlic cloves, crushed
Pinch of salt
1 tbsp Bart Medium Curry Powder
5 dried (or fresh) curry leaves
2 tomatoes, roughly chopped
Black pepper
500ml (1pt) chicken or vegetable stock
400g (14oz) leftover cooked turkey (or chicken), shredded
260g (9oz) pack spinach
2 x 250g (9oz) packs microwave basmati rice
Squeeze lemon juice

1 Put the lentils in a bowl, cover with cold water and set aside.
2 Fry the onion, ginger and garlic, adding a pinch of salt, for 8 mins until turning golden. Stir in the curry powder, curry leaves, tomatoes and a grind of black pepper. Cook for 2 mins.
3 Drain the lentils and add to the pan, along with the stock and 250ml (½pt) cold water. Bring to the boil, then simmer for 20 mins until the lentils are soft.
4 Stir in the turkey and spinach, cover and cook for 3-4 mins, until the spinach is wilted.
5 Prepare the rice according to pack instructions.
6 Season the curry to taste and add a squeeze of lemon juice.

www.waitrose.com/recipe

2021 year-to-view calendar

JANUARY

M		4	11	18	25
Tu		5	12	19	26
W		6	13	20	27
Th		7	14	21	28
F	1	8	15	22	29
Sa	2	9	16	23	30
Su	3	10	17	24	31

FEBRUARY

M	1	8	15	22	
Tu	2	9	16	23	
W	3	10	17	24	
Th	4	11	18	25	
F	5	12	19	26	
Sa	6	13	20	27	
Su	7	14	21	28	

MARCH

M	1	8	15	22	29
Tu	2	9	16	23	30
W	3	10	17	24	31
Th	4	11	18	25	
F	5	12	19	26	
Sa	6	13	20	27	
Su	7	14	21	28	

APRIL

M		5	12	19	26
Tu		6	13	20	27
W		7	14	21	28
Th	1	8	15	22	29
F	2	9	16	23	30
Sa	3	10	17	24	
Su	4	11	18	25	

MAY

M		3	10	17	24	31
Tu		4	11	18	25	
W		5	12	19	26	
Th		6	13	20	27	
F		7	14	21	28	
Sa	1	8	15	22	39	
Su	2	9	16	23	30	

JUNE

M		7	14	21	28
Tu	1	8	15	22	29
W	2	9	16	23	30
Th	3	10	17	24	
F	4	11	18	25	
Sa	5	12	19	26	
Su	6	13	20	27	

JULY

M		5	12	19	26
Tu		6	13	20	27
W		7	14	21	28
Th	1	8	15	22	29
F	2	9	16	23	30
Sa	3	10	17	24	31
Su	4	11	18	25	

AUGUST

M		2	9	16	23	30
Tu		3	10	17	24	31
W		4	11	18	25	
Th		5	12	19	26	
F		6	13	20	27	
Sa		7	14	21	28	
Su	1	8	15	22	29	

SEPTEMBER

M		6	13	20	27
Tu		7	14	21	28
W	1	8	15	22	29
Th	2	9	16	23	30
F	3	10	17	24	
Sa	4	11	18	25	
Su	5	12	19	26	

OCTOBER

M		4	11	18	25
Tu		5	12	19	26
W		6	13	20	27
Th		7	14	21	28
F	1	8	15	22	29
Sa	2	9	16	23	30
Su	3	10	17	24	31

NOVEMBER

M	1	8	15	22	29
Tu	2	9	16	23	30
W	3	10	17	24	
Th	4	11	18	25	
F	5	12	19	26	
Sa	6	13	20	27	
Su	7	14	21	28	

DECEMBER

M		6	13	20	27
Tu		7	14	21	28
W	1	8	15	22	29
Th	2	9	16	23	30
F	3	10	17	24	31
Sa	4	11	18	25	
Su	5	12	19	26	

RELAX & UNWIND

Dolly daydream

Writer Marion Clarke and **Yours** *readers remember the dollies we used to love to pretend to mother*

There was nothing I loved more than taking my doll Jennifer for a stroll. She was my favourite Christmas present that year and I was heartbroken when she accidentally fell off my bed as I was dressing her and suffered severe damage to her pretty china head. Despite promises to send her to a dolls' hospital, she was never repaired, and I never had another doll that I loved quite as much.

Valerie Bell must have been a more careful little girl than I was, because she still has Rosebud, a present from her grandma when she was six: "She no longer says 'Mama', but other than that she is in remarkable shape. She still has her original clothes and opens and closes her eyes. Rosebud knows all my secrets (which she is very good at keeping) and these days she sits in my living room on her own cushion and stool."

Half the fun of having a doll was dressing her - or him - in nice clothes, as **Dorothy Pluck** recalls: "Every Christmas my girl doll got a lovely new outfit. After she was sure my sister and I were sound asleep, Mum sat up late happily sewing away on her Singer treadle machine.

"I desperately wanted a little brother so one year my doll had a sex change and Mum dressed her as little boy. I named him George Ernest. My sister called her doll Rosaleen and we had great fun making up stories about them. George Ernest was a ship's captain and he married Rosaleen in one of our games." And we're sure they lived happily ever after, Dorothy!

Mary Tyler's first doll was given to her as a present at a children's Christmas party: "She was in a plain cardboard box and had no clothes on which horrified my Auntie May! She knitted her a complete outfit with a red coat and hat. Knitting didn't come naturally to Auntie May so the outfit was all the more precious. I called my doll Caroline and cherished her, taking her to bed with me each night.

"When I was 12 I decided I was too old for dolls so I packed her away carefully, intending to give her to my own little girl one day. When I did that, 20 years later, I found Caroline abandoned at the bottom of the toy box along with Tiny Tears and Sindy so I rescued her and stowed her away again." That's a sad tale, but hopefully a granddaughter will come along soon to cherish Caroline as young Mary did.

In the Sixties, Barbie and Sindy were at the top of every little girl's wish list. Advertised as 'the doll you love to dress', Sindy was **Chris Wileman's** best present in 1965: "My Sindy was a brunette and her every outfit was a child's dream come true. As well as everyday clothes she had sports clothes, glamorous outfits and accessories."

Heather Moulson used to spend all her Christmas money on outfits for her Sindy doll: "She had a striped jumper and jeans and white plastic shoes as well as her own bed and dressing table.

"One day when my friend

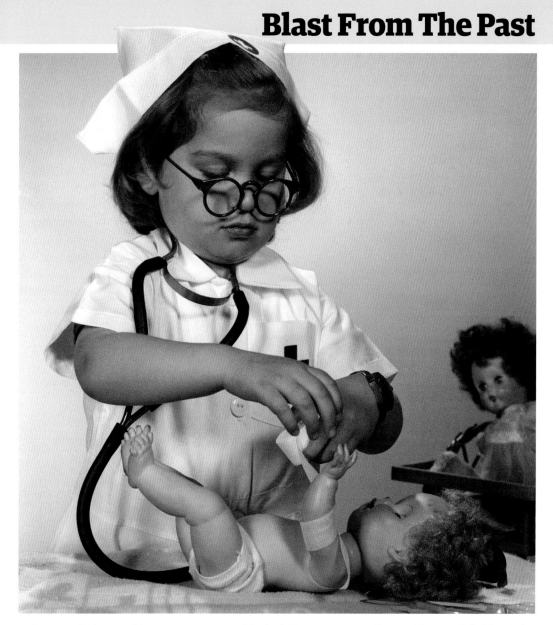

and I were playing outside, a dog picked Sindy up in his mouth and ran off with her. I was inconsolable. My mum put a card in our local shop window appealing to the dog's owner to return her. Soon after, when I came home from school, there she was, placed behind the milk bottles on our doorstep."

Margaret Anderson's doll Susan came to a sorry end when she was left in the airing cupboard while the family were away on holiday and the hot water tank leaked. Margaret says: "I can't remember how long it was before I stopped crying!"

Being the youngest in the family, most of **Diane Shearn's** toys were hand-me-downs from her older siblings so she was thrilled to be given a brand-new Pedigree doll which she called Pimpy. Sadly, Pimpy was made of rubber which gradually disintegrated after years of play and cuddling, but the story has a happy ending: "60 years later I was browsing in an antique shop when I spotted a familiar-looking

box. Inside was a dolly identical to my beautiful Pimpy in perfect condition!"

"I loved Christmas because it always brought me a new doll," writes **Sylvia Foster**. "My favourite was Tressy because her hair grew and I liked styling it. I was very upset when I pressed her tummy one day and her hair failed to wind back in, but my dad had a look and fixed it for me."

Good old dad to the rescue - I only wish mine had been able to mend poor Jennifer!

GET THE PICTURE

We've put someone in disguise – who could it be? To find out, you'll have to solve all the clues. When you've finished, read the letters in the coloured squares to reveal their name (5, 5).

Across

1 Wound mark (4)
5 Embassy employee (8)
11 Fuse metal together (4)
12 Long-term (illness) (7)
13 A few (4)
14 Come into view (6)
17 Octopus arm (8)
18 Leg joint (4)
19 Holds up (6)
20 Money on account (6)
23 Zone (6)
24 Rubs harshly (6)
26 Irritates (6)
29 Subtle shade of meaning (6)
30 Job (4)
32 Case, example (8)
33 Barren region (6)
36 Flavouring plant (4)
37 Sanction (7)
38 Acting part (4)
39 Spinal bone (8)
40 Rewards with cash (4)

Down

2 Move furtively (5)
3 Crest of high ground (5)
4 Happen (5)
6 Inborn (6)
7 Taciturn (7)
8 Blunder (7)
9 Worried look (5)
10 Overcome (6)
14 Assistants (5)
15 Bird with a huge bill (7)
16 No matter who (7)
21 Find new accommodation for (7)
22 Case for the accused (7)
25 Perfume (5)
26 On fire (6)
27 Autumn month (7)
28 Earnest (7)
30 Easily chewed (6)
31 Frighten (5)
33 Reside (5)
34 Waste metal (5)
35 Race with a baton (5)

Puzzles

QUIZWORD

Across

1 Who replaced Carol Vorderman as Countdown's 'numbers girl' in 2009? (6, 5)

9 Who is Maya - - -, the American poet and author of I Know Why the Caged Bird Sings? (7)

10 Who is - - - Doolittle, the Cockney flower girl featured in Pygmalion and My Fair Lady? (5)

11 Which surname can link Marti, Sidney and Sarah? (4)

12 In the Dickens novel A Christmas Carol, what is Tiny Tim's family name? (8)

14 & 22A In the classic film The Third Man, which character was played by Orson Welles? (5, 4)

15 Buckingham is the home of which leading public school? (5)

20 Who was the original presenter of the BBC's Question Time? (5, 3)

22 See 14A

24 Who is Kiran - - -, the 2006 Man Booker Prize-winning author of The Inheritance of Loss? (5)

25 What title was held by German princes who were members of the college which chose the Holy Roman Emperor? (7)

26 Which flowers were the subject of approximately 250 paintings by Monet? (5, 6)

Down

2 Quadratic equations are used in which branch of mathematics? (7)

3 See 19D

4 Which Paris museum is accessed via a glass pyramid? (6)

5 What completes The Bourne - - -, the first of the film trilogy starring Matt Damon? (8)

6 & 18D In 1915, which British nurse was executed in Belgium by the Germans? (5, 6)

7 What is an Islamic legal pronouncement? (5)

8 Valletta is the capital of which Mediterranean country? (5)

13 Which wheelchair-bound TV detective was played by Raymond Burr? (8)

16 Who was Sir Frank - - -, pioneer of the jet engine? (7)

17 What is Madrid's premier museum and art gallery? (5)

18 See 6D

19 & 3D Which Texan-born model had a long-term relationship with Mick Jagger and is the mother of four of his children? (5, 4)

21 Which southern Iraqi city, on the Shatt al-Arab is the country's main port? (5)

23 Which 19th-century prime minister founded the British police force? (4)

Were you right? Turn to page 182 for the answers

Beside the cherry

Stella is looking forward to moving to the country, but will be sorry to leave behind treasured parts of the past

By Helen M Walters

I stood by the cherry tree in the garden and sipped my coffee. It was my favourite place to come when I needed to think. I knew I wouldn't be able to do it for much longer. The house was on the market and we were headed for a new life in the country. My husband, Greg, was going to be managing holiday cottages and I was finally going to concentrate on my art. There was a lot to look forward to, and yet ...

"What are you thinking?" my husband asked.

I leaned into him for a hug.

"You're thinking about how much you're going to miss the garden, aren't you, Stella?" he said, reading my mind as usual.

He was right. We'd planted the cherry tree just after we'd moved in five years ago and I'd loved watching it grow as our marriage grew. I felt bereft at the thought of not seeing it every day. We had talked about trying to dig it up and take it with us, but I was worried it might die. And that was even worse than leaving it behind.

There was another reason as well. My eyes drifted towards the pile of stones beside the cherry tree that marked the spot where my beloved cat, Tabby, was buried. Leaving her behind was going to be a terrible wrench as well.

It was three years since she'd died - run over on the road by an impatient driver going too fast. Even

tree

"The future was looking bright. I couldn't let sadness over things lost get in the way"

After so many years of waking up to the noise of traffic, it was strange waking up to birdsong.

"Hey, Sleepyhead, come out into the garden," Greg said.

"Why?" I asked.

"I've got something for you," he said, heading downstairs.

I pulled on jeans and a sweater, wondering what all the excitement was about.

The garden was soft with dew as I walked over to where Greg was standing, looking pleased with himself.

As I got closer I saw he had planted something. It looked like a stick.

"Look at the label," he said.

I crouched down to look.

"It says Stella," I looked up at him and smiled.

"Yes," he said. "I didn't realise Stella was a type of cherry until I went to the garden centre. But what could be better to welcome you to your new home."

"Thank you," I said. It might only look like a stick now, but it would grow and eventually would be as lovely as the one we left behind. It might take years, but that didn't matter. This was our forever home. I wanted to grow old here.

Looking at the tiny cherry tree every day would help me focus on the future and not dwell on the past.

Two weeks later I stood with my coffee and contemplated the cherry tree. It hadn't grown yet but was looking good as it stood in the quiet serenity of the garden.

Meanwhile, we'd settled into the new house. Greg had started his new job and I'd begun to set up the outbuilding that was going to be my studio. I'd even started to think that this far from any main roads I might be able to overcome my fear of having a cat.

I'd even dropped a couple of hints to Greg about it, but he hadn't picked up on them, probably because he was too busy with his job.

"Hey, Stella," Greg called across the lawn to me. "Close your eyes."

Wondering what he was up to, I did as I was told.

Then, suddenly, I knew. I felt a small furry bundle in my arms and opened my eyes to a very cute, fluffy kitten reaching up to my face.

Greg had picked up on my hints after all.

"She's called Cherry," he said.

Before I could stop, tears were pouring down my face. But this time they were tears of pure joy.

thinking about it brought bitter tears to my eyes.

Greg had asked me many times whether I wanted to get a new cat, but I'd always said no. The road seemed to get busier with traffic, and I couldn't risk another cat meeting the same fate as Tabby.

I finished my coffee and we headed back into the house to continue decluttering. Glancing over my shoulder at the cherry tree I felt a pang of regret, then I shook it off. The future was looking bright. I couldn't let sadness over things lost get in the way.

Three months later and the morning sunshine crept in through the curtains as I turned over in bed, taking a while to register where I was.

Baby, I can drive

Writer Marion Clarke and **Yours** *readers recall the highs and lows of tearing up L-plates and failing driving tests*

THE HIGHWAY CODE

HMSO 25p net

It took several attempts and three patient instructors before I finally passed my driving test. And, luckily for me, that was before they introduced the extra hurdle of a written exam as well as executing a perfect three-point turn without hitting the kerb!

That tricky manoeuvre was **Mrs S Rose's** downfall: "All was going well until I drove onto a quiet road and was asked to do a three-point turn. I got flustered and it slowly became an eight-point turn, by which time a queue of cars had formed as their drivers waited for me to stop zig-zagging wildly back and forth. I finally managed to drive away, very red-faced, knowing I had failed."

Happily, Mrs Rose passed on her second attempt, but it took **Mooneen Truckle** four goes before she could throw away her L-plates: "My youngest daughter was still a toddler and I had to take her with me on my lessons. There were no seatbelts in those days and she used to sit on the back seat cuddling her teddy, as good as gold. More often than not, she landed on the floor when we did an emergency stop but she just picked herself up and climbed back on to the seat."

When **Anne Dunford's** husband taught her to drive, the whole family piled into the car: "Children in the back, hubby in the passenger seat and myself behind the wheel. We lived down a lane and the only way was up – a hill start! Each time we nearly got away when, whoops, the engine stalled. At last, with a great flurry of gravel and spinning wheels we'd get away, waving to the neighbours who had been waiting to see us go by." Anne finally got the hang of driving when her

friend took over as instructor – proving once again that your husband teaching you to drive is not a good idea.

After one too many arguments, **Olive Parry's** husband paid for her to have seven proper lessons: "At £1 a lesson, would you believe? I passed first time and in 42 years never had an accident."

At the other end of the scale, **Rosemary Leedham** was a slow learner: "I had about 100 lessons before I passed my test. I found it difficult to understand how to change gears and had a bad habit of wandering on to the wrong side of the road. After I passed, my friends and family weren't too keen on driving with me – except for my gran, who said that as she'd had her life it wouldn't matter if she were in an accident!"

My sympathies are with the driving instructors as they have a tough job, especially with learners like **Kathy Blundell**: "On my first lesson,

your car

the instructor explained about the mirror and the pedals and told me I wasn't to worry as he had dual control. Off we went. He said, 'Don't go too fast! Slow down'. I replied indignantly, 'You're the one with the pedals, I'm only learning'."

Carol Keates had a more helpful teacher: "Being only 5ft tall, seeing over the steering wheel and reaching the pedals were a challenge! My driving instructor had two wooden blocks that he put under the seat to tilt it forward. That wouldn't be allowed now!"

After Carol failed her test twice due to nerves, her instructor came up with another idea: "He advised me to contact my GP who obliged by prescribing a sedative to help me through the next test. Duly relaxed, I sailed through. But when the examiner asked me to sign the pass form, my hands were shaking so much I couldn't write, so I guess the 'sedative' was only a placebo - but it did the trick!" The mind boggles at how things might have gone if Carol's doctor had actually prescribed a dose of Valium...

Whenever **Wendy Chappell** asked her instructor if she could take the test, his answer was always, 'I don't think you are quite ready yet'. "The final straw came on the day I reversed the car into a ditch. He left me to go in search of a telephone box. When he came back, we had to wait another half an hour for the breakdown truck to reach us.

"At the time I had a very strict boss and I asked the instructor if he would drop me back at work. Fortunately, when I dashed in 40 minutes late and said I had to be pulled out of a ditch, she roared with laughter.

"I have never driven since, but at least I've reduced the number of potential casualties!"

Bumping into

It seemed Megan's trip to the supermarket had ended in disaster - or was it a chance to start again?

By Margaret Skipworth

Megan glanced at her watch. Justin was due home in 20 minutes and she still had no idea how she was going to explain the big dent in his Ferrari.

'I could tell him the truth,' she thought. 'I could say, "Justin, darling, I fancied some chocolate last night and as there wasn't any in the house I had to go to the supermarket. I couldn't find my car keys, so I took the Ferrari. Trouble is, I sort of reversed into another car."'

Megan rolled her eyes. She knew, whatever she said, Justin would go ballistic when he saw the mess she'd made of his precious car.

Megan had been married to Justin for five years. But any feelings she had for him had been eroded by his affairs. He was a fashion designer and, several times a year, he travelled to Milan and Paris on 'business trips' with his PA, Courtney -

who was also his latest girlfriend.

Megan had seen them together when she was shopping. They looked like a perfect couple, holding hands and snuggling up to one another. As soon as she got home that day, Megan tugged off her wedding ring. Justin didn't even notice.

"Why don't you leave him?" Her sister, Emily, had asked for the umpteenth time when they met for lunch recently. Emily had been happily married for ten years and was an incurable romantic.

"I'm OK. I live in a nice house. I have nice things." Megan took a sip of wine. "As long as I go with Justin to fancy restaurants with his posh clients, he doesn't mind how I spend the money."

"For goodness' sake, Meg. Money's not everything," Emily snapped.

"Please, Em, don't mention that word: love." She heaved a huge sigh. Her parents had been 'in love'

Brian

but eventually got divorced; her friend's husband had an affair on their honeymoon; and Megan herself had been jilted, at the altar, by her fiancé. Love meant nothing to her. She reached across the table and squeezed Emily's hand. "Honestly, Em, I'm not interested in love. I'd rather have money to give me security and the freedom to do as I please."

Dragging her mind back to the present, Megan tried to think of a plausible story about the Ferrari. But her thoughts keep drifting back to the incident at the supermarket...

While she was inspecting the damage to the cars, a man appeared. "Are you all right?" he asked.

"Is this your car?" she stammered.

"Never mind about the car," he said, taking off his jacket and slinging it round her shoulders. "You're shivering."

Megan managed a weak smile. "I'm fine." She was shaken up but she couldn't help noticing that his mist-grey eyes swam with kindness.

"The damage doesn't look too bad," he remarked after checking the cars. "My friend owns a garage. He'll..."

"I'd rather take the car home," Megan blurted out, imagining Justin's reaction if the Ferrari wasn't on the drive.

"No problem. I'll sort that out." He gave her a warm smile. "Then, I'll call a taxi and take you home."

When the taxi pulled up outside the house, Megan invited him in for coffee. They sat and chatted comfortably, like old friends, for a couple of hours. Megan learned his name was Brian and he was a geography teacher.

She didn't mention she was married and he didn't say anything about a wife.

Before he left, he wrote his number on his shopping receipt. "Call me if you need any help with the car," he said.

"What on earth has happened to my car?" Justin thundered through the door. The sickly-sweet smell of Courtney's perfume swirled through the house.

"You know you can't go out in the Ferrari..." Justin stormed into the kitchen.

Megan wasn't listening as she thought of Brian and felt for the receipt with Brian's number in her pocket. She realised then that she would swap all Justin's money for another evening with a man as considerate as Brian.

Her lifestyle with Justin suddenly seemed tacky and meaningless. It seemed, like Emily had assumed, that she'd lost her way in what she really wanted from life. But who better to help her get her life back on track than a geography teacher? The thought made her giggle.

"Have you been drinking?" Justin glared at her. "Is that how you crashed the car?"

Megan took a deep breath. "It was like this, Justin darling. I just fancied some chocolate." She flashed him her sweetest smile. "So I drove your Ferrari to the supermarket."

Justin's eyes widened.

"And guess what?" She strides purposefully towards the door. "I bumped into a gorgeous guy called Brian. Goodbye."

DILEMMA

Fit these words into their correct places in the grids below.

3 LETTERS	4 LETTERS	5 LETTERS	ESTATE
BOW	CAFE	ACORN	FIASCO
BUS	CODE	ADOPT	FRACAS
DAB	CUFF	ADORE	
EAR	FETE	AUDIO	**7 LETTERS**
EBB	GLUE	AROMA	STOPGAP
EVE	IDLE	AUDIT	STRUDEL
FED	IDOL	SLANG	
FEE	LIMB	TOAST	**9 LETTERS**
FOE	OAST		DAREDEVIL
ORE	OILY	**6 LETTERS**	DECEITFUL
STY	ONCE	BANGLE	
TWO	ORAL	CHERUB	**11 LETTERS**
USE	TALE	DAMSEL	CONDITIONAL
VIA	YOGI	DANGLE	
VIE		DONATE	

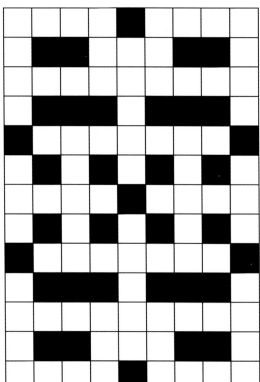

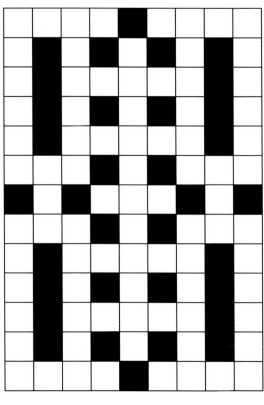

QUICK CROSSWORD

Across

3 Crime investigator (9)
8 Castle's ditch (4)
9 Single man (8)
10 Clothing (6)
13 Chinese mafia (5)
14 Telepathic (7)
15 Fish eggs (3)
16 Riled (7)
17 Error, slip (5)
21 Substance used to curdle milk (6)
22 The - - - of Venice, play (8)
23 Chances quoted by a bookmaker (4)
24 Child's jumping toy (4, 5)

Down

1 Neutral, unbiased (9)
2 Casing for a small explosive (9)
4 Cinder (5)
5 Fence in (7)
6 Family ancestry chart (4)
7 Fine brandy (inits)
11 Bedfordshire zoo (9)
12 Physicist, eg (9)
14 Long narrow seed case (3)
15 Withdraw (7)
18 Large lorry (5)
19 Reject (4)
20 Sound rebound (4)

Were you right?
Turn to page 182
for the answers

The man for

Harry Noakes is nervous about his job interview, especially when the questions turn rather strange

By Viv Doyle

Harry entered the council offices feeling nervous. He'd not had a job interview for many years but his wife, Joan, had been encouraging. "You're perfect for the job, and you don't deserve to be on the scrap heap yet," she'd said.

Harry went up to the young girl on reception and gave her his name. She glanced at her list. "Room 14, Mr Noakes. Upstairs, third floor. You'll be called when Mr Morgan's ready for you."'

Harry found room 14 and sat on the chair outside, uncomfortable in his best grey suit. It had come out of mothballs for the occasion, but Joan had sorted it out and ironed his new shirt for him.

"You look a real treat, love," she had said as she kissed him goodbye.

"I'm more comfortable in overalls," he'd replied.

Harry had enjoyed being a school caretaker, but the old buildings were being demolished and the school was merging with another. This new school caretaker job had come up just at the right time. Thank goodness Joan had spotted it in the local paper. For her sake, he hoped he would get this job. Much as she loved him, he knew she didn't want him sitting around at home all day.

The door opposite opened, and a man beckoned him in.

"I'm Peter Morgan, chief executive," the main introduced himself. "And this is my assistant, Mr Beckonsworth." He looked through the papers on his desk, frowning. "We don't seem to have your application here, Mr Noakes." He turned to Beckonsworth. "See if Janice can lay her hands on it, will you?"

After he'd gone, Mr Morgan said, "While we're waiting, you can tell me about yourself. Are you working at the moment?"

"Yes, but I've been given redundancy notice by the council."

"And how long have you been in your present post?"

"Twenty-three years."

"Oh my!" The thick grey brows shot up. "No use asking if you've got the right experience then!" He gave a friendly laugh. "What would you say was the most difficult part of your job?"

Harry pondered. He and Joan lived in a bungalow next to the school, so he was sometimes called out in an emergency. He knew it was part of the job and Joan, bless her, had never once grumbled.

"Being on call day and night, I suppose."

"We operate a rota. You're entitled to some time off. You have a clean driving licence, I presume?"

"Oh yes. And I'm qualified to drive a minibus."

"We use vans, Mr Noakes."

Harry was puzzled. 'Surely they didn't use vans to drive the kids around?' he thought.

"Well some of the little blighters run rings around you so you have to be one jump ahead of them all the time"

"So tell me what you like about the job."

Harry reflected. His confidence grew as he remembered Joan saying that the Head had told her he'd been a great asset to the school and wished him well. He knew he had an excellent reference. What a shame Mr Morgan didn't have it in front of him.

"I like the variety," he began. "Every day's different and there's never a dull moment!"

Mr Morgan's smile was almost conspiratorial. "Indeed! There are plenty of challenges. Now, tell me about your pet hates?"

"Well some of the little blighters run rings around you so you have to be one jump ahead of them, all the time." Mr Morgan nodded, sagely, as Harry went on. "But I always say prevention is better than cure. If you can guess what they'll be getting up to next, that's half the battle."

"Yes, I suppose so. They can do a lot of damage if left unchecked."

the job

"Natural born vandals, some of 'em."

"Er . . . quite. Now there will be some re-training involved. I don't know what methods you've been using, but we make use of state-of-the-art technology here. We've gone ultrasonic!"

"Ultrasonic?" Harry's head was spinning.

The door opened and Beckonsworth entered. "I'm sorry, Mr Morgan, there's been a mix-up!" he gasped. "The girl in reception today is on work experience. She sent Mr Noakes to the wrong room."

Mr Morgan looked aghast. "What job did you apply for, Mr Noakes?"

Harry frowned. "School caretaker, of course." To his dismay, both men burst out laughing. "Why, what job is this?"

Mr Morgan spluttered, pulling out a handkerchief. "Pest control!"

Harry could see the funny side of it too but, as he got up he swallowed his disappointment and apologised for wasting their time. Still, what a story he'd have to tell Joan!

Then, to his surprise, Morgan waved him back down again.

"Stay where you are Mr Noakes. With all your experience of controlling human pests, you could well be the best man for the job!"

Sun, sand and sangria

Writer Marion Clarke and **Yours** *readers relive their travellers' tales of holiday firsts*

For many readers their first holiday abroad was their honeymoon.

For their honeymoon in 1957, **Irene Philp** and her husband chose a tour to Innsbruck. After meeting their travel rep in London, they proceeded to Folkestone: "We boarded the steamer and it was one of the worst Channel crossings ever. It took three hours to reach Calais. The boat tossed and turned and I was petrified. All that could be heard was the crashing of crockery and glass in the bar."

Thankfully, things improved after that: "We made our way to the special train that was waiting for us. Dinner in the dining car was magical. The tables were beautifully set with little lamps on each one, almost like the Orient Express."

Rosemary Medland didn't fare too well on her first Spanish holiday: "After a coach ride on a narrow mountain road in pouring rain, we arrived at our hotel to find that the roof leaked. The bar staff made us mugs of hot chocolate to warm us up, but we were frozen all week and asked for extra blankets on our bed. We were disappointed when we returned home to find that there had been a heatwave!"

For **Freda Ellen Minns**, her first holiday abroad in 1954 was truly romantic. "I was 19 and my boyfriend, Tommy, asked my parents if he could take me to Switzerland. They said yes! When we reached Lucerne, he took me to a jeweller's shop to buy an engagement ring and I chose an amber topaz. The staff gave us Champagne and wished us happiness. That evening, Tommy took me to a nice restaurant and put the ring on my finger.

As we walked up the path to our hotel it was lit by glow-worms and all the stars were out. We were married for 51 years."

Blast From The Past

Mrs G Raper also has idyllic memories of her first time abroad to celebrate her tenth wedding anniversary in 1972: "Our hotel in Lloret de Mar was fantastic. We had a huge room with a lovely balcony and during the day we paddled in the warm sea, stopping for coffee and liqueurs outside a bodega. In the evening we sat around the pool listening to a guitarist."

Aged 19, **Linda Mills** was apprehensive at the prospect of going on a cruise with her friend: "We flew to Genoa (my first time on a plane) and my nerves did not improve when the pilot announced that we had to get off again due to engine trouble! We boarded the same plane an hour later and boy, was I scared."

However once on their cruise liner in Naples, Linda got into the swing of things. "We went to Athens and climbed the acropolis; the view from the top was breath-taking. The weather was so hot that my friend passed out. I remember sipping iced tea in Egypt with the pyramids behind me and the sphinx in front and feeling like someone in an Agatha Christie mystery." Travel can broaden the mind in unexpected ways, as **Eileen Bowman** learned when she first went to Menorca aged 60 and hired a car: "We came to traffic lights showing red. Looking in the mirror, I saw that the driver of the car behind was making hand gestures telling me to move forward slightly to activate the lights. I did so and, lo and behold, they turned to green and off we went."

It was the bedding that puzzled **Sally Ketley** when she went to the picturesque village of Arzl in the Tyrol: "It was our first encounter with a duvet and we thought we had to unbutton it and climb inside. The chambermaid saw our dilemma and gave us a demonstration, including how to air it over the balcony rail in the morning."

When **Marie Claire Orton** came to England to stay with a penfriend, it was our eating habits that surprised her: "I felt embarrassed when I didn't like the food, or drinking tea. My penfriend's schoolmates were amazed when I told them that we drank table wine with our school meals in France!"

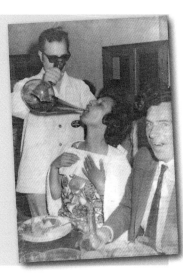

Wendy Chappell and her new husband went to Majorca where their dream of a romantic getaway became a little tarnished: "Our hotel was disappointingly basic and there was another hotel being constructed next door. The builders worked at odd times, arriving in the evening and banging away for several hours.

"However, we were able to go on lots of trips including a jolly evening barbecue where the sangria flowed freely. A jug was passed round and we had to drink from the spout without spilling any - an impossible feat for me!"

Man's best

Sophie would love to move in with Gavin, but her boyfriend's dog isn't having any of it

Sophie snuggled closer to Gavin on the sofa but as K9 gave a low growl she leapt away.

"K9!" Gavin scolded, ruffling the top of the Labrador's head. "Be nice to Sophie."

'Nice!' thought Sophie. 'That dog is never nice. He hates me.'

If they went out for a walk and K9 went for a swim, it was Sophie he shook his wet coat all over.

If she and Gavin tried to sit together on the sofa, K9 wriggled his way between them and showed Sophie the whites of his eyes if she protested.

If she cooked in Gavin's kitchen, K9 would lay on the floor making it impossible for Sophie to get around. No, being nice was not something you could accuse K9 of.

"What am I going to do?" Sophie had asked her best friend, Jan. "We want to move in together, but Gavin can't ever stay in my flat because my flatmates don't like K9 and the dog is making it impossible for me to stay at Gavin's."

"Have you tried food?" Jan asked. "That's

"You'd think K9 would be used to me by now. But no, he's man's best friend. Literally a woman hater"

---

usually the way to a dog's heart."

"I'm not sure K9 has a heart," Sophie muttered. "I've bought him treats, but he won't take them from me."

"Walks?" Jan asked.

"He won't come out with me. Only if Gavin comes too. Last week I had to drag 30 kilos of reluctant Labrador home when Gavin had to go out. People stopped to laugh at us."

Jan was laughing too.

"The only other thing is time," she said.

"I've given it nearly two years," Sophie protested. "You'd think K9 would be used to me by now. But no, he's man's best friend. Literally a woman hater."

Jan was now doubled over with laughter. Sophie glowered.

She was still smouldering when she went around to Gavin's that evening. Maybe she should call the relationship a day. It just wasn't working, and she didn't think Gavin could choose between her and K9.

She walked around the corner, passing a house being renovated and stopped suddenly.

A tiny sound was coming from the skip outside. A cold tickle ran down her spine and Sophie gripped her handbag tighter. Could it be rats?

She almost hurried on but then she heard the squeak again. Very gingerly she peered inside the skip. On top of piles of wood, an old armchair and loose bricks was a fairly new cardboard box. The sound was coming from that. She stretched over and pulled the box towards her. Inside there were three little kittens huddled together.

"Oh, you poor things," she murmured, scooping the box up and hurrying to Gavin's house.

"Look what I found in the skip," she said breathlessly.

Sophie held out the box to Gavin who took it just as K9 pushed his way into the conversation, sniffing at t.

"Don't let the dog near them." Sophie said panicked.

"Ah, look K9," Gavin said. "Kitties."

"Gavin! He'll hurt them."

"No, he won't. What are we going to do with them though?

"I hadn't thought about that," Sophie replied. "But I couldn't leave them there overnight. I'll take them to the rescue centre in the morning."

By Alyson Hilbourne

friend

"They're probably hungry," Gavin said, peering in the box.

"Yes, right, you look after them while I nip to the shop and get some kitten food."

Sophie went out of the door, her heart beating fast. She was back in five minutes and let herself in with the key.

"I've got—" she began but stopped at the most extraordinary sight.

K9 was laid on the living room floor with Gavin beside him. The three kittens were nestling up to K9's chin and climbing over each other to get on his face.

"Told you he'd be fine with them," Gavin said.

All evening K9 lay with the kittens. He watched them eating the kitten food from a plate without interfering. He allowed them to romp all over him and licked them contentedly, He didn't even growl at Sophie when she snuggled up with Gavin.

"He's a changed personality," Sophie said. "Perhaps we should keep the kittens."

Gavin pulled a face.

"We can't keep three kittens, Soph."

"How about one then?"

The next morning Sophie took two kittens to the rescue centre and borrowed a small crate for the kitten they'd decided to keep, which they named Simba. He would be safe in there while they were out at work. A few weeks later, when she was certain K9 and Simba were the best of friends she returned the crate to the rescue centre.

"I'm moving into Gavin's," she told Jan happily.

"What about K9?" Jan asked.

"A reformed character," Sophie said. "No longer man's best friend. He's totally in love with our kitten, Simba."

RUNAGRAM

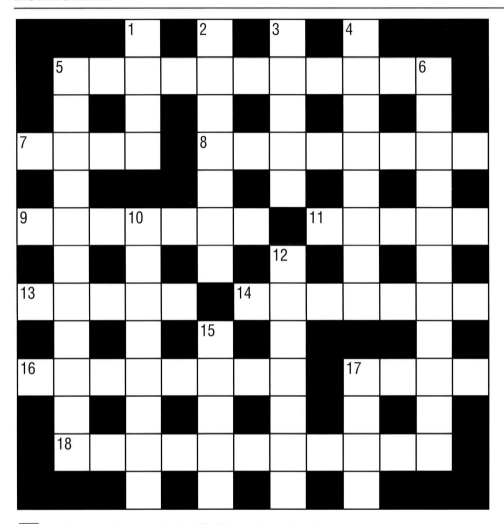

E ach clue contains a straight definition and a series of consecutive letters which, when rearranged, will form the answer. The clue 'You're doing it to ARM GUN RAIDERS (8)' gives you RUNAGRAM, for example.

Across

5 Large Belgians produce something to nap in (8, 3)
7 Visit naughty relation (4)
8 Renting out gas (8)
9 Spin beats many cricketers (7)
11 We ban obscene comic (5)
13 Start feeling better (5)
14 The most remarkable celestial bodies (7)
16 Ballot for a game (8)
17 He wrote music for Danish cabarets (4)
18 It helps discover the truth of elected Tories (3, 8)

Down

1 Soft leather fabric (4)
2 Sharpens new tool (7)
3 They bite legs at night (5)
4 Some tools become defunct (8)
5 Seagull roasted for a snack (7, 4)
6 Shopkeeper in Greece or Gretna (11)
10 Host likes teaching pub game (8)
12 Lewd fellow's plump (4-3)
15 Bar keeps a type of cook (5)
17 Wash each table (4)

MISPRINTS

Oops! Someone's having a bad day! Each of the clues for this crossword contains a typing error. Your task is to find where the incorrect letter lies in each case and correct it in order to answer the clue.

For example, **1 Across** should read *'One who makes up dances for theatre'* and the answer is *Choreographer.'*

Across
1 One who makes up lances for theatre (13)
8 Unable to love due to the cold (4)
9 Extremely fit (5)
10 Height-loss plan (4)
13 Stinks out (9)
16 One who wishes with a rod (6)
18 Spiky plait (6)
19 Stake surrounded by seats (5)
20 Coat extracting industry (6)
22 Spanish fish (6)
27 Type of nun from down under? (9)
30 School vest (4)
31 Move fervently (5)
32 Fluorescent fight (4)
33 Property of being equally skilful with each wand (13)

Down
2 Where clarity begins? (4)
3 Travels around a planer (6)
4 Bring out of manger (6)
5 Lease a stage (4)
6 Barn made from rabbit fur (6)
7 Green capital (6)
11 Moody plant (4)
12 White boat cheese (4)
14 Secret service spa (5)
15 Set of steps built over a hall (5)
17 Old unwanted sloth (3)
18 Sporting cat (3)
20 Wooden hamper (6)
21 Builder of the biblical arm (4)
23 Having little or no pain (4)
24 Burn up at a meeting? (6)
25 Bike feat (6)
26 Talking bard (6)
28 Cultivate sand (4)
29 Warden of England (4)

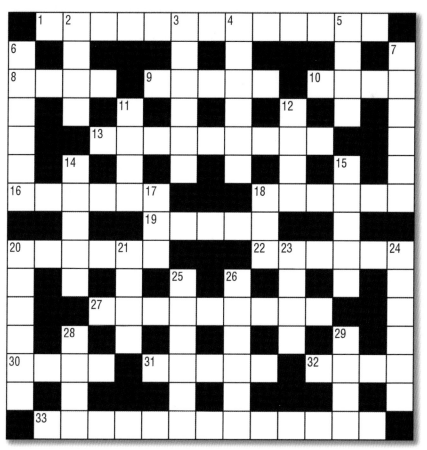

Were you right? Turn to page 182 for the answers

Waves of nostalgia

It's a bittersweet moment for Daisy being back in the place she

Daisy walked down the field, taking her time, breathing in the fresh, crisp air.

There it was, the sea glittering away in the sunlight. She'd missed it ever so much.

It must have been at least ten years since she was last here. They said you should never go back, just to keep the memories alive as so many things change. But Daisy knew it was different for her. She looked at the whole world with new eyes every day now.

From where she stood, Daisy could see the library where she used to work. She could recall the days when she used to rush out of her flat, giggling with her friends as they raced down the street.

And there was the town hall where she first learned to dance. It hadn't been long before her teacher had recognised she had a gift for ballet and as she grew older, her life had revolved around studying, working and dancing.

She had pirouetted through her life in this beautiful seaside town and happily pursued her dream until it was shattered by one moment, taken from her on a day when the clouds had darkened and her steps had faltered on her path to being a professional ballet dancer. Then life was never the same again.

A bark disturbed Daisy from her reminiscing and suddenly she came face to face with a speckled face with a lolling tongue. A springer spaniel had appeared from nowhere and proceeded to jump up at her with excitement as if she were a long-lost friend.

"Benjy, where are you?" she heard from afar.

Daisy crouched to give the dog a little pat and when she rose, she found herself looking into

By Rebecca Mansell

> **"Just for a moment she held her breath as the memory came flooding back"**

loved so much

twinkling, blue eyes.

"Hello! There isn't normally anyone here at this hour of the morning."

Daisy smiled. Didn't she know this man? His good looks were vaguely familiar, and she found herself instantly warm to him.

"It's the best time of the day," she replied softly.

"You here on holiday?" asked the stranger, throwing a ball for Benjy.

Daisy shook her head as she watched the spaniel race after the ball and when he returned, he dropped the ball at her feet, looking up expectantly.

The man laughed. "He likes you."

"He's very friendly," chuckled Daisy, and she picked up the ball and attempted to throw it but it didn't go far at all. Nevertheless, Benjy jumped

onto it with frenzied energy.

They both laughed.

"I'm Tony, by the way. I've lived here all my life. Never found a reason to leave."

Daisy nodded with understanding.

"I'm Daisy," she admitted with a smile. "I used to live here but..."

Her voice trailed off feet.

"I think I remember you," said Tony softly, breaking the uneasy atmosphere. "I saw you dance once."

"You did?" Daisy was surprised.

Not many people knew who she was. Her 'fame' only lasted seconds really. One moment she was regarded as possibly the best ballet dancer in the world and then next, she retreated into the shadows, leaving people to only whisper about her disappearance.

"But you don't remember me, do you?" Tony spoke again.

'Did she know him?' she wondered. Perhaps they went to school together.

"I was there that day, on the bridge."

His words were soft and just for a moment she held her breath, as the memory came flooding back.

She'd been rushing to meet her friend Sally, to tell her she was going to London to star in Swan Lake when her steps had faltered, she'd felt like she was going to faint. Overcome with dizziness, she longed to sit down but there was nothing she could do but lean on the wall of the bridge. Panic had surged through her body, with a frightening pain in her legs until at last rescue had come. A friendly man helped her off the bridge.

"I think my mind has tried to forget," she said quietly.

He nodded. "I understand. How are you now?"

Benjy circled around them, his tail wagging frantically.

"I am much better, thank you."

And she was. Now she could venture out again. It had taken years and it had been like learning to walk again. But here she was, right where she was meant to be.

She was to start teaching ballet soon, in the very town she had always loved. She couldn't wait to get started.

They returned to gazing at the view.

"I am here, every morning, at this time," spoke Tony quietly.

Daisy smiled as she felt a feeling of happiness swirl within her.

"It's the best time of the day," she replied.

Memories taste

*Writer Marion Clark and **Yours** readers open the larder door to reveal their favourite childhood foods*

Food nostalgia floods us with such vivid memories of people and places from our past. Childhood Sunday lunches of crisp roast chicken – soft, white meat bathed in 'Aahh' Bisto with over-cooked carrots and watery cabbage, followed by a dessert of tinned fruit cocktail and a thin slice of Lyons vanilla-block ice-cream.

Later, because there was always room, a tea of tinned red salmon sandwiches was followed by snuggling up by the fire watching Black Beauty on our two-channel telly.

Everyone has a favourite or, in some cases, a detested dish, which transports them back to a particular moment of their lives.

Reading about the meals you grew up with, I couldn't help wondering which foods today's children will recall with such fuzzy warmth in years to come... spag bol or a processed cheeseburger, maybe? I'm willing to bet that good old bread and dripping won't be high on their list, but

for **Barbara Errington** it was a gastronomic treat: "A slice of Mam's homemade bread spread with pork dripping and plenty of brown jelly from the bottom of the basin, sprinkled with a little salt and pepper."

Elisabeth Richards reckons that children today would never eat her favourite dish, known as sop: "It was bread soaked in tea and sugar with a bit of butter added. Sounds awful, but it filled a hungry belly when there were a lot of us to feed."

Margaret Greenaway reminds us that not everyone has rose-tinted memories of home cooking for very good reasons: "My dad was away in India and life was tough for me and Mum. Food was nothing to get enthusiastic about. Bread dipped in an Oxo drink, toast with horrible margarine, skinny sausages with a few chips."

Growing up in Norfolk, **Pauline Frost** fared better: "Mum always cooked hot, nourishing dinners ready for when we arrived home from school. We had rabbit pie with lovely thick gravy, tripe, vegetable hotpot, pig's trotters and homemade brawn. For dessert we loved Yorkshire pudding served with treacle."

Vera McGrath was also lucky enough to have a mother who was a good cook: "She made

a lovely rabbit soup with homemade dumplings and eel with fresh parsley sauce and mashed potato."

Many of you wrote about meals that were always associated with a particular day of the week. And, in the case of **Abbi Kinsella's** family, always on time! "Sunday dinner was at 1pm and Sunday tea at 5.30pm. Tea consisted of salmon and cucumber sandwiches, jelly, trifle, Carnation evaporated milk and, best of all, sliced cucumber and onion which was soaked in vinegar the night before."

Sunday teatime meant winkles for both **Valerie Reilly** and **Sharron Radford**. Sharron writes: "Using a pin, it would take about an hour to carefully prise enough winkles out of their shells to cover one slice of bread and butter. Sprinkle some vinegar and it was worth every mouth-watering minute!"

Valerie's father knew how to raise a laugh: "Dad was always a bit of a comedian and he used to cover his face with the small black covers from the shells saying they were beauty spots."

For Saturday lunch, **Diane Hutton's** mother used to dish up fried lamb's brains, tossed in flour and served on toast: "Delicious then, but I wouldn't fancy them now!"

of this

The Monty Python team may have written a song to celebrate it, but like Marmite, Spam is loved or hated. **Heather McEwen** is in the latter camp: "I recall with dread the day I was given Spam fritters for school dinners."

While **Anne Ridgely** thought the opposite: "When I was at school, the best dinner was Spam fritters, mash and beans. I still like them to this day."

Spam is still sold, but many of you wrote about foods that aren't available now. **Eileen Bolton** said the food she misses the most is the tinned blackcurrant purée that her mother put in blackcurrant jelly.

Sue Wooldridge still remembers Lyons' individual fruit pies, which were unusually square in shape and filled with apple and blackcurrant.

Pam Kwiatkowski would like to know what happened to her favourite pudding, Cremola, and Jo Masters still has fond memories of the pud. "When my grandmother collected me from school and gave me lunch, the dessert was Cremola, a cross between egg custard and crème caramel. Delicious."

Doreen Smith remembers a time when getting a takeaway didn't mean phoning for a pizza: "On Wednesdays after school Mam would send me and my brother to the local butcher's shop with two bowls and tea towels. The butcher would fill the bowls from two big pots of pease pudding and hot faggots and we would rush home to eat them."

A cake-up call

Tess has had enough of being taken from granted by her family

As Tess mixed the ingredients for her cake, she thought about her own mixed emotions of resentment, anger and amusement, stirred up by thoughts of the past and the present.

As she baked, her 16-year old son Josh sprawled out on the sofa, earplugs in, listening to his phone, while Phoebe, 18, was on her laptop upstairs, out of sight. Dave, her husband, was out at the football match, which explained the speedy birthday meal, eaten hurriedly between him getting home from work and meeting his football mates.

Tess hadn't actually wanted to celebrate her birthday in quite such a rush, but as usual she went along with it. It's also why she went along with baking her own birthday cake. After all, she'd grown used to life being not how she'd once imagined it. There wasn't any one specific thing to blame for how things were; it was more a creeping apathy, slowly spreading over the entire family so that she ended up doing everything.

With the cake in the oven, Tess stepped outside to better appreciate the early spring sunshine. The garden was showing glimpses of what was to come, all the results of her own efforts.

She sighed, thinking about the problem. Their home had become a landing stage, a feeding station, a sleeping refuge; somewhere to get your washing done. No-one saw it as a home anymore, even Tess. But today she'd had enough. Her birthday marked a milestone. Something had to happen.

The day had begun no differently to any other. As usual, she was the first up, going quietly down to the kitchen to make breakfast and put on a load of laundry. On the table were three different envelopes. How fitting, she thought, that her family knew the kitchen table would be the most likely place she'd find them.

By John Darley

The first card from Dave was suitably predictable, in that it was the very same one he'd chosen last year. Keeping with tradition. Phoebe's card came with a present. The sentiments in the card attempted to show feelings which were sadly lacking in the toiletry set she'd purchased complete with anti-ageing cream.

And Josh? Well, at least the footballers on his card wore the colours of his and Dave's supported team, although, in Josh's case, the support came more from the sofa.

Their thoughtlessness was almost ironic. Her children cared on a global scale about climate change and world injustice and were passionate about many causes but anything - or anyone - close to home seemed to count for nothing.

As for Dave, his passions nowadays were more directed towards the beautiful game than for his once-beautiful wife. She had been a looker back then and he'd certainly looked, but it seemed over time he'd taken his eye off the ball.

> **"Their home had become a feeding station; somewhere to get your washing done. Something had to happen"**

The oven timer sounded and Tess returned to the kitchen. The cake was baked. It was time.

Lighting the candles, Tess walked into the living room with the cake, starting off a rousing rendition of 'Happy Birthday'.

"Shall I make a wish?" she asked. Nobody answered. She blew out the candles and began cutting the cake.

"I can't eat all that," protested Dave, as Tess piled the huge portion onto his plate. There were similar protests from her children, but Tess ignored them all.

"What about you Mum," said Phoebe, "you've only got a sliver."

"Have I? Oh yes. Never mind. All the more for you."

"But this is way too much," interjected Josh.

"Just try a bit. For me, please."

"I don't even know if I'll be able to lift it," said Dave who, for once, wasn't being sarcastic.

Tess watched as they gingerly lifted their huge slices to their lips. Once bitten into, their reaction

was unanimous.

"That's disgusting!" spat out Dave.

"It's gross!" from Josh.

"What's in it?" demanded the more practical, yet equally revolted Phoebe.

Tess grinned. "Not what you expected?"

"What's in it?" repeated Phoebe.

"Food for thought."

Later that evening, as they all sat together eating pizza and watching episodes of The Great British Bake Off, Tess explained her reasoning for putting gravy and salt into the cake mix.

"The surprising taste was to remind you never to take anything - or me - for granted."

A strong atmosphere of humble pie pervaded her loved ones. And she did love them.

"Pizza okay?" said Dave.

"Fine," Tess said. "And so is everything else." 'For now,' she thought. "But be warned, you can't just have your cake and eat it."

Not that any of them would be planning to do so, any time soon.

QUICK CROSSWORD

Across
1 Road-building machine (5, 6)
9 Peter - - -, snooker star (5)
10 Frog sound (5)
11 Infant (3)
12 Coat (of paint) (5)
13 Porridge ingredient (7)
15 Martin - - -, TV actor (6)
17 Office (6)
20 Dappled (7)
23 Leather strip (5)
25 Fury (3)
26 Unclothed (5)
27 Helicopter blades (5)
28 Autonomous, separate (11)

Down
2 Cuddly toy bear (5)
3 Liverpool racecourse (7)
4 Church of England clergyman (6)
5 Lawful, legal (5)
6 Call up (5)
7 Substitute (11)
8 Underhand dealing (11)
14 Ruin (3)
16 Negative (3)
18 Spoke (7)
19 Fit to be eaten (6)
21 Voucher (5)
22 Shelf (5)
24 Repeatedly (5)

Puzzles

CORNER TO CORNER

To the right

1 Luck (7)
2 Cricketer's implement (3)
3 Bog fuel (4)
4 Not, either! (3)
5 Large sailing vessel with three masts once used as a warship (7)
6 Large striped cat (5)
7 Mesh (3)
9 Suffer illness (3)
11 Become peaceful (6)
13 University site (6)
14 Carpenter's tool (3)
16 Assist (3)
19 Tar (7)
21 Smash into fragments (7)
24 Bird's claw (5)
26 Tree's juice (3)
28 Rotate (4)
29 Small dog's bark (3)
31 Can (3)
33 1988 comedy film starring Tom Hanks (3)

To the left

2 Feather scarf (3)
3 Capital of France (5)
4 John - - -, star of Bergerac and Midsomer Murders (7)
5 Indian state (3)
6 Classic Scottish kilt pattern (6)
7 Zero (3)
8 Fail to care for (7)
10 Golfer's peg (3)
12 Wander (4)
15 Label, flap (3)
17 Quick little bite (3)
18 Fool (4)
20 Normal, average (7)
22 Garbage container (7)
23 Hurry (6)
25 Perth's river (3)
27 Shiny fabric (5)
30 Floor cleaning implement (3)
32 - - - cushion, sewing box item (3)
34 Clothesline fastener (3)

Were you right?
Turn to page 182
for the answers

The best view in the world

Zara longs to show her husband the place that takes her breath away

By Patsy Collins

So many times over the last couple of years, Zara had loved to walk her dog Toffee up Portsdown Hill. A place of solace whenever her husband Jayden was away with the navy, she would always pause at the top to take in the wonderful view of the sea. It was calming and reassuring. But best of all, whenever she looked out at this view, she always imagined what bit of sea Jayden was looking at just at that moment, whether it was an exotic vista in the Caribbean or a boring, functional port.

Often Jayden would email Zara pictures of places he visited. Sometimes he sent postcards. Always he'd tell her what he'd seen and done, by text, phone call or in person when he returned. And she loved to hear about every little detail.

Before they'd moved near Portsmouth, Zara and Toffee's regular walks were in areas Jayden knew well, so she'd had no need to describe them to him. But having only moved a few years ago, the view from Portsdown Hill was one he'd never seen in person. So whenever she went there, Zara noted all the small details to tell Jayden about. "I saw wild orchids today," she'd text. Or, "there were people flying kites, I might try that myself."

The view from Portsdown Hill included the city of Portsmouth, the Isle of Wight and The Solent that lay between them. Sometimes the sea was

a calm blue reflection of a cloudless sky, while at other times it was so dark it seemed bottomless. From her spot on Portsdown Hill, Zara saw yacht races, drifting cruise ships or occasionally her husband's ship sailing in.

"It's the best view in the world," she told Jayden.

When he was next home, he teased her a little, suggesting other places they could walk Toffee. "I don't want to go up Portsdown Hill yet," he told her. "I'm saving the best until last!"

It wasn't a problem. Zara was happy walking along the seafront with him, or through the rose gardens at Southsea. Toffee was even more easily

pleased. Having both his humans home was enough excitement, even if they just walked him down the shop for a pint of milk or throw him a ball in the garden.

Over his years in the navy Jayden had seen fascinating sea creatures, moored within sight of the Sydney Opera House, and been surrounded by icy wonderlands. He'd helped in rescue missions, defended coastlines and taken part in international operations.

"You might be disappointed after all the amazing things you've seen," Zara said. "Somehow I doubt it," he replied.

The morning they were finally headed to Portsdown Hill, they set off early. The sun hadn't yet burned through the morning mist and the dull boom of ship's foghorns followed them as they climbed.

"I don't suppose you don't enjoy that sound," Zara said. "But I find it comforting. When you're away, it reminds me that there's safety precautions helping ensure you come back to me."

"There are more pleasant sounds on a ship," Jayden told her. "A pipe to say there's mail to be collected or that we can go ashore, especially when we're back in Portsmouth and I know you'll be waiting for me on the jetty."

Toffee, as usual, was torn between racing after the rabbits he hadn't a hope of catching and staying close with Zara and Jayden. They were so engrossed with talking over plans, watching Toffee, and paying attention to where they placed their feet on the steep, slippery path, they didn't realise that the early morning mist had become quite dense fog until they reached the spot where Zara always stopped to look.

Below them, in every direction, was nothing but swirling white. It was impossible to see anything else.

Jayden turned to Zara. "The best view in the world?" he said with a cheeky grin.

"Not exactly," Zara laughed. "Much as I love it when there's actually something to see, that's not what I meant when I said it was the best view in the world. For me, it's so wonderful because this is the perfect place that I can see your ship coming into harbour, meaning it's time for me and Toffee to walk home and come and meet you. It's always such a thrill, this place has come to mean a lot to me."

"You're right," Jayden replied. "This isn't the best view in the world, nor is anything I've seen while I've been away." He gently held her face in his hands. "This right here with you smiling at me, that's the best view in the world."

Our forever

*Writer Marion Clarke and **Yours** readers remember the cuddly dogs and loyal cats that were such a special part of our childhoods*

Our family Labrador, Danny, never accepted that he was too big to be a lapdog, despite often trying to get comfortable on our knee. Dad reckoned he had a cheeky sense of humour because when told to 'sit' before crossing a road, Danny would promptly obey - but with his back to the traffic, making the person on the other end of the lead look pretty silly!

Like Danny, **Freda Minns'** dog Jack loved to join in family life: "I liked to dress him up and take him for a walk in my doll's pram. As he got older he liked to play football with my brothers. When it was our mealtime, mam would say to Jack, 'Go and fetch the children' and Jack would run down the road and bark to let us know the food was ready.

"He used to go every day to the butcher's shop for his bone. When he got it, he went 'woof, woof' to say thank you."

When we were growing up, it was not unusual to see dogs going out on their own, as **Janice Baldwin's** Butch did: "He was very clever and used to take himself off for a walk down the local high street. He waited patiently at the pedestrian crossing until a car stopped for him - and he knew which shops would give him a biscuit!

"He loved children and would wait for them to come out of school. They all knew him and rushed to give him a hug. Sometimes they would knock on the door to ask if Butch could come out to play. He'd trot off with them and come home when he'd had enough. After he died, my father never had another dog."

Named Rinty after the film star RinTinTin, **Pauline Baldwin's** first dog was a black-and-white mongrel who also liked to roam the neighbourhood: "My mother discovered that there was a round of people he regularly visited. She was embarrassed to discover he was fed at some of these houses and at one of them he was given steak! He was fed well at home too so definitely wasn't hungry."

Di Aston was just a baby when she had her first cat: "Timmy (full name, Timothy Whiskers Aston) was three months older than me and we grew up together. He was better than a guard dog any unwelcome visitor to my pram was sent off with a flea in their ear!

"He grew to be the most handsome, biggest, yet gentlest of tabby cats. He let my sister and me dress him up and push him around in a doll's pram."

Eddie Quayle had a more unusual pet, a bantam hen called Chirpy: "She was one of two chickens but her brother sadly died so she was taken under my wing and spoilt rotten. She became very tame and would follow me into the house. I took her blackberry picking and she came back with a purple beak from all the ones she had eaten.

"Chirpy was an excellent mother - she hatched out

friends

drops of brandy. He lived a long time for a goldfish although we suspect he was probably pickled!"

When I was a girl, I longed to have a parrot that could talk like Kiki in Enid Blyton's Adventure Series, but the budgerigar that **Valerie Reilly** won in a raffle sounds great fun, too: "We named him Peter and I spent a lot of time singing nursery rhymes to him. He would dance along the bottom of his cage, nodding his head and singing 'Half a pound of tuppenny rice' before screeching 'Pop goes the weasel' as loud as he could.

"He had a replica budgerigar on his perch that he called Jerry after hearing my mother call my dad's name. When we took all his toys out to clean his cage, Peter called out, 'Where's Jerry? Where's Jerry?'"

During the war, **Elizabeth Thompson** had a chatty budgerigar, also called Peter: "He never failed to say 'Don't forget your gas mask!' every time I went out."

ducklings as well as chicks. When the ducklings made straight for the water, she didn't know what to do as she wasn't keen on water herself."

Even children who didn't have any other pets might win a goldfish at the fair. **Vicky Bagley** gave hers the original

name of Goldy: "He did well until my little niece decided to feed him milk, juice and the occasional dolly mixture. We would find him floating on his side on the surface of his bowl, one fin waving weakly.

"My mum sorted him out by submerging him in fresh tap water in the sink and adding a few

Cleaning up

Emma's literally in the dumps after a recent break-up but then a trip to her nan's changes her outlook completely

Emma looked around her flat. Clothes were draped over chairs, shoes kicked into corners, and every coffee mug she owned was on a surface somewhere. Emma's shoulders slumped.

It hadn't been like this when James was here. Together they had kept the place clean. She went to the kitchenette and glared at the sink, full of pans resting in stagnant water. James was long gone, never to return, and there seemed little point tidying up.

"This is all your fault, James," Emma muttered as she groped in the cupboard for a clean mug, failing to find one. She couldn't raise the enthusiasm to wash up. It was a waste of a weekend doing chores and she couldn't think of anything worse than standing over a kitchen sink washing up right now.

Instead she drove the mile across town to go to her nan's house. Pulling into the drive usually brought Nan to the door but today there was no cheery greeting. Emma knocked and waited. Then

---

"Today the kitchen looked like a horror movie... chairs were overturned and flour was tipped over the work surfaces"

---

she knocked a little harder.

Frowning, she turned to the key safe, and entered the numbers to get Nan's spare key.

She opened the door and stepped into the hall. She peered into the living room, but it was empty. The kitchen door at the end of the hall was shut. Emma closed the front door and froze as she heard bangs and crashes coming from the kitchen.

Something definitely wasn't right.

The hairs on the back of her neck rose and her mouth went dry. Emma tiptoed forward but as she got to the door she heard a man's voice, low

and threatening.

"Get out, you silly old bird. Get out!"

This was followed by the sound of something heavy falling on the floor.

Emma wanted to open the door, but she couldn't move. Her heart was racing. She was just reaching for her phone when a crash snapped her into action to fling open the door.

"Gran!" she shouted.

One look at the kitchen and Emma knew something was terribly wrong. Gran was immensely proud of her house and kept everywhere polished and shining. Not a jar or cup was normally out of place.

Today, though, the kitchen looked like a horror movie. The back door and windows had been flung open wide, chairs were overturned, and flour was tipped over the work surfaces creating a white mist. Several saucepans were on the floor and drawers had been opened randomly. Muddy footprints tracked from the back door.

But most telling of all was Gran's handbag that had been upended, spilling lipstick, boiled sweets and loose change on to the draining board.

Emma was just about to step into the room when she noticed she wasn't alone. A man, half hidden by the tea towel he was holding up, stepped out from the larder.

"Where's Gran?" she yelled. "What have you done with her?"

The man blinked several times.

"Gran?" he frowned.

"My grandmother. Mrs Williamson," Emma's voice rose to a shriek.

"Oh." The man looked relieved. "She's gone upstairs to find a net curtain."

Emma flashed him a look of disbelief and edged back to the hall.

By Alyson Hilbourne

"Gran?" she yelled towards the stairs. "Are you up there?"

Footsteps sounded overhead and then on the stairs.

"Told you," the man said with a grin. "Did you think I'd done away with her?"

"What are you doing here?" Emma scowled.

At that moment her grandmother walked in.

"I see you've met Kieran, my gardener," her Nan said, giving her a hug. "We've been trying to get a blackbird out of the kitchen after he followed Kieran inside for a coffee." She looked around. "It's made a huge mess."

Kieran gave Emma broad smile, which despite her best efforts, made her heart suddenly turn somersaults.

"Kieran Grant," he said, sticking his hand out.

His tanned face made his blue eyes stand out. Emma took his hand, which made her legs feel like jelly.

"Emma. Granddaughter. I just came for coffee."

"Excellent," Kieran said. "You can help me tidy up now the blackbird has left. Look! There it is. On the fence." He pointed out the door to a blackbird with a beady eye.

Gran clapped her hands.

"I'll put the kettle on. I've got a cake for you when you're finished. We can go out in the garden to have it and share the crumbs with that bird."

Kieran threw Emma a sponge with a smile that made her forget she had sworn off men after James.

Some days just don't go as planned, Emma mused, sweeping the flour into a pile, but then she wasn't sure she minded that very much after all.

Puzzle answers

GET THE PICTURE PAGE 150

Across 1 Scar, 5 Diplomat, 11 Weld, 12 Chronic, 13 Some, 14 Appear, 17 Tentacle, 18 Knee, 19 Delays, 20 Credit, 23 Sector, 24 Chafes, 26 Annoys, 29 Nuance, 30 Task, 32 Instance, 33 Desert, 36 Herb, 37 Endorse, 38 Role, 39 Vertebra, 40 Pays.

Down 2 Creep, 3 Ridge, 4 Occur, 6 Innate, 7 Laconic, 8 Mistake, 9 Frown, 10 Defeat, 14 Aides, 15 Pelican, 16 Anybody, 21 Rehouse, 22 Defence, 25 Scent, 26 Alight, 27 October, 28 Sincere, 30 Tender, 31 Scare, 33 Dwell, 34 Scrap, 35 Relay. Hidden celebrity Lenny Henry.

QUIZWORD PAGE 151

Across 1 Rachel Riley, 9 Angelou, 10 Eliza, 11 Webb, 12 Cratchit, 14 Harry, 15 Stowe, 20 Robin Day, 22 Lime, 24 Desai, 25 Elector, 26 Water lilies.

Down 2 Algebra, 3 Hall, 4 Louvre, 5 Identity, 6 Edith, 7 Fatwa, 8 Malta, 13 Ironside, 16 Whittle, 17 Prado, 18 Cavell, 19 Jerry, 21 Basra, 23 Peel.

DILEMMA PAGE 158

QUICK CROSSWORD NO.1 PAGE 159

Across 3 Detective, 8 Moat, 9 Bachelor, 10 Attire, 13 Triad, 14 Psychic, 15 Roe, 16 Angered, 17 Lapse, 21 Rennet, 22 Merchant, 23 Odds, 24 Pogo stick.

Down 1 Impartial, 2 Cartridge, 4 Ember, 5 Enclose, 6 Tree, 7 VSOP, 11 Whipsnade, 12 Scientist, 14 Pod, 15 Retract, 18 Artic, 19 Veto, 20 Echo.

RUNAGRAM PAGE 166

Across 5 Sleeping bag, 7 Aunt, 8 Nitrogen, 9 Batsmen, 11 Beano, 13 Begin, 14 Meteors, 16 Football, 17 Bach, 18 Lie detector.

Down 1 Felt, 2 Spanner, 3 Gnats, 4 Obsolete, 5 Sausage roll, 6 Greengrocer, 10 Skittles, 12 Well-fed, 15 Baker, 17 Bath.

MISPRINTS PAGE 167

Across 1 Choreographer, 8 Numb, 9 Obese, 10 Diet, 13 Protrudes, 16 Angler, 18 Cactus, 19 Arena, 20 Mining, 22 Paella, 27 Macadamia, 30 Exam, 31 Adore, 32 Neon, 33 Ambidexterity.

Down 2 Home, 3 Orbits, 4 Rescue, 5 Exit, 6 Angora, 7 Athens, 11 Tree, 12 Feta, 14 Agent, 15 Stile, 17 Rag, 18 Cap, 20 Mallet, 21 Noah, 23 Arid, 24 Attend, 25 Saddle, 26 Parrot, 28 Farm, 29 Kent.

QUICK CROSSWORD NO.2 PAGE 174

Across 1 Steam roller, 9 Ebdon, 10 Croak, 11 Tot, 12 Layer, 13 Oatmeal, 15 Clunes, 17 Bureau, 20 Mottled, 23 Thong, 25 Ire, 26 Naked, 27 Rotor, 28 Independent.

Down 2 Teddy, 3 Aintree, 4 Rector, 5 Licit, 6 Evoke, 7 Replacement, 8 Skulduggery, 14 Mar, 16 Not, 18 Uttered, 19 Edible, 21 Token, 22 Ledge, 24 Often.

CORNER TO CORNER PAGE 175

CORNER TO CORNER
To the right 1 Fortune, 2 Bat, 3 Peat, 4 Nor, 5 Galleon, 6 Tiger, 7 Net, 9 Ail, 11 Settle, 13 Campus, 14 Saw, 16 Aid, 19 Bitumen, 21 Shatter, 24 Talon, 26 Sap, 28 Spin, 29 Yap, 31 Tin, 33 Big.

To the left 2 Boa, 3 Paris, 4 Nettles, 5 Goa, 6 Tartan, 7 Nil, 8 Neglect, 10 Tee, 12 Roam, 15 Tab, 17 Nip, 18 Twit, 20 Regular, 22 Dustbin, 23 Hasten, 25 Tay, 27 Satin, 30 Mop, 32 Pin, 34 Peg.